PLCs at Work®

and the IB

PRIMARY YEARS PROGRAMME

Optimizing Personalized, Transdisciplinary Learning for All Students

EDITORS

TIMOTHY S. STUART • DAVID (CAL) CALLAWAY

RIANNE ANDERSON • DAVID (CAL) CALLAWAY • CALLEY CONNELLY
LAURA JO EVANS • YODIT HIZEKIEL • EYERUSALEM KIFLE
KACEY MOLLOY • JACQUELINE OLIN • TIMOTHY S. STUART

Solution Tree | Press

a division of
Solution Tree

555 North Morton Street
Bloomington, IN 47404
800.733.6786 (toll free) / 812.336.7700
FAX: 812.336.7790

email: info@SolutionTree.com
SolutionTree.com

Visit go.SolutionTree.com/PLCbooks to download the free reproducibles in this book.

Printed in the United States of America

Library of Congress Cataloging-in-Publication Data

Names: Stuart, Timothy S., editor. | Callaway, David, editor.
Title: PLCs at work and the IB primary years programme : optimizing
  personalized, transdisciplinary learning for all students / editors,
  Timothy S. Stuart & David (Cal) Callaway ; contributors, Rianne
  Anderson, David (Cal) Callaway, Calley Connelly, Laura Jo Evans, Yodit
  Hizekiel, Eyerusalem Kifle, Kacey Molloy, Jacqueline Olin, Timothy Stuart.
Description: Bloomington, IN : Solution Tree Press, [2022] | Includes
  bibliographical references and index.
Identifiers: LCCN 2022036764 (print) | LCCN 2022036765 (ebook) | ISBN
  9781954631151 (paperback) | ISBN 9781954631168 (ebook)
Subjects: LCSH: International Baccalaureate Primary Years Programme. |
  Professional learning communities. | Interdisciplinary approach in
  education. | Academic achievement.
Classification: LCC LB1731 .P55 2022 (print) | LCC LB1731 (ebook) | DDC
  370.71/55--dc23/eng/20220921
LC record available at https://lccn.loc.gov/2022036764
LC ebook record available at https://lccn.loc.gov/2022036765

Solution Tree
Jeffrey C. Jones, CEO
Edmund M. Ackerman, President

Solution Tree Press
President and Publisher: Douglas M. Rife
Associate Publisher: Sarah Payne-Mills
Managing Production Editor: Kendra Slayton
Editorial Director: Todd Brakke
Art Director: Rian Anderson
Copy Chief: Jessi Finn
Senior Production Editor: Suzanne Kraszewski
Content Development Specialist: Amy Rubenstein
Acquisitions Editor: Sarah Jubar
Copy Editor: Evie Madsen
Proofreader: Elisabeth Abrams
Cover and Text Designer: Fabiana Cochran
Associate Editor: Sarah Ludwig
Editorial Assistants: Charlotte Jones and Elijah Oates

Acknowledgments

We would like to thank our children, Tyler, Ian, Moriah, Tyr, and Lex, who have inspired us to keep learning about learning. This book is a humble attempt to share some of our learning with a larger audience. Thanks for putting up with us.

Mona and Ligita, you continue to support, challenge, and refine our crazy ideas and epiphanies. You make us better educators and people.

To our colleagues and contributing authors, Rianne Anderson, Calley Connelly, Laura Jo Evans, Yodit Hizekiel, Eyerusalem Kifle, Kacey Molloy, and Jacqueline Olin: this book is a testament to your knowledge, skills, and dispositions in the areas of elementary school education and Professional Learning Communities at Work®. Your work will inspire thousands as it has inspired us.

Solution Tree Press would like to thank the following reviewers:

Janet Gilbert
  Principal
  Mountain Shadows Elementary School
  Glendale, Arizona

Rosalind Poon
  Vice Principal 8–12
  Richmond School District
  Richmond, British Columbia, Canada

Ringnolda Jofee' Tremain
  K–8 Principal
  Trinity Leadership Arlington
  Arlington, Texas

Table of Contents

Chapter 6
The Educational Assistant in the PYP and PLC 121
Eyerusalem Kifle

Chapter 7
Leading Change in the PYP Through PLCs. 139
Calley Connelly

Afterword 157
Timothy S. Stuart and David (Cal) Callaway

Index 159

About the Editors

Timothy S. Stuart, EdD, is a regional education officer for the U.S. Department of State's Office of Overseas Schools. Dr. Stuart formerly served as head of school of the International Community School of Addis Ababa, Ethiopia. He was formerly executive director of strategic programs at Singapore American School. In this role, Dr. Stuart served as the chief architect for research and development to support strategic school reform. He is the former high school principal of Singapore American School and Jakarta International School. Dr. Stuart has been an international and cross-cultural educator since 1991, serving schools in Ethiopia, Turkey, Switzerland, Indonesia, and Singapore and on a Navajo reservation in New Mexico in the United States.

Dr. Stuart is the coauthor of the books *Personalized Learning in a PLC at Work, Children at Promise,* and *Raising Children at Promise.* He is the editor and a contributing author of the anthology *Global Perspectives: Professional Learning Communities at Work in International Schools* and is a contributing author to *It's About Time: Planning Interventions and Extensions in Secondary School.* Dr. Stuart's research and writing reflect his passion for creating optimal school environments so all students can learn and engage at the highest levels.

Dr. Stuart holds a doctorate from Seattle Pacific University, a master's degree from the College of New Jersey, and a bachelor's degree from Wheaton College. As a child, Stuart lived and attended schools in France and Germany.

To learn more about Timothy S. Stuart's work, follow @drtstuart on Twitter.

David (Cal) Callaway, EdD, is the deputy head of school at the International Community School (ICS) of Addis Ababa in Ethiopia. Dr. Callaway's move to the ICS was to join its forward-thinking and innovative team that works to support all students through personalized learning and the professional learning community (PLC) process. Dr. Callaway has worked in international education since 1998. He worked as an elementary, middle, and high school teacher before working in administration, first as a director of technology and then as a Primary Years Programme (PYP) coordinator, before settling in as an elementary principal. Dr. Callaway has worked in international schools in England, China, Latvia, and Ethiopia.

Dr. Callaway is a member of the National Association of Elementary School Principals, which in 2021 awarded him National Distinguished Principal in recognition of his work as an elementary principal since 2016. Additionally, the elementary school at the ICS was awarded Exemplary PLC status in 2021 through his team's work in driving learning with the PLC process. Dr. Callaway strongly believes in an inclusive approach to education and has adapted learning support services to work closely with students in a PLC.

Dr. Callaway has presented on co-teaching learning communities, educational environments, and personalized learning for the Central and Eastern European Schools Association (CEESA) and as part of PLC institutes in Africa. He previously worked as a copy editor for the Investment and Development Agency of Latvia (LIAA) and was an editor for a Netherlands embassy–commissioned book on Dutch-Latvian historical relationships.

Dr. Callaway received a bachelor's degree from the University of St. Andrews in Scotland, a postgraduate certificate in education from Oxford University, a master's degree from the University of London, and a doctorate in educational leadership from Wilkes University in Wilkes-Barre, Pennsylvania.

To learn more about David (Cal) Callaway's work, follow @tyrcal on Twitter or visit www.linkedin.com/in/dr-david-cal-callaway-87652799 on LinkedIn.

To book Timothy S. Stuart or David (Cal) Callaway for professional development, contact pd@SolutionTree.com.

Introduction

Timothy S. Stuart and David (Cal) Callaway

The world has changed significantly since the turn of the 21st century, with especially dramatic change happening because of the global COVID-19 pandemic. These changes have caused educators and researchers alike to reconsider the value of a traditional education. Are schools, both individually and as part of national systems, equipping students with the knowledge, skills, and dispositions they most need for futures in this changed world (Facer, 2021)? As education leaders, we must reassess how we lead and organize our school systems to ensure we are doing the best we can to support all students. The one-size-fits-all approach to education is no longer an acceptable pedagogy, either morally or professionally; traditional school structures are failing to achieve the goals of both excellence and equity (Eaker & Marzano, 2020). Educators must shift toward a more personalized approach to education that considers individual student needs. This shift requires a culture of continuous improvement in which leaders pay attention to changing both school structures and school culture.

We propose that this shift in approach to education is most effective in the primary years with the implementation of the International Baccalaureate Primary Years Programme (IB PYP), a highly effective, learning-progressive approach.

The Primary Years Programme

The IB PYP is based on three pillars—(1) the learner, (2) learning and teaching, and (3) the learning community—that surround a central core of student agency (International Baccalaureate Organization [IBO, 2018]). These three pillars are the primary elements of importance that educators in a PYP should consider when thinking about the way they approach teaching and learning in their school.

The Learner

The first pillar—*the learner*—addresses learning from the student perspective, including the outcomes students should seek for themselves (IBO, n.d.c). The important focus is on students taking action and having agency, which form the backbone of the learning-progressive element, giving students the opportunity to take ownership of their own learning (Stuart, Heckmann, Mattos, & Buffum, 2018).

Learning and Teaching

The second pillar—*learning and teaching*—focuses on articulating the process of learning and teaching within the PYP, including ideas of *transdisciplinary learning* (a curriculum-organizing approach that extends beyond the limits of individual subjects) and methods for learning skills, making inquiries, and solidifying conceptual understanding (IBO, n.d.c). This aspect of the program clearly lays out the foundations of a guaranteed and viable curriculum (what all students will learn in the allotted time; Marzano, Norford, Finn, & Finn, 2017) to ensure the work done in schools has clear outcomes that support students' futures.

The Learning Community

The third pillar—*the learning community*—covers aspects related to international mindedness, which is an overarching construct related to intercultural understanding, global engagement, and multilingualism (Hacking et al., 2017). The learning community pillar of the PYP further emphasizes collaboration, technology, and the social outcomes of learning and how school communities can support these outcomes (IBO, n.d.c).

These three interrelated pillars culminate in students having agency to take action in their learning through choice, voice, and ownership—the ultimate representation of effective student agency. By taking individual and collective action, students come to understand the responsibilities associated with being internationally minded and appreciate the benefits of working with others for a shared purpose (IBO, n.d.c).

History and Growth

The IB PYP was introduced in 1997 following the introduction of the Middle Years Programme in 1994 and the Diploma Programme in 1968. The former International Schools Curriculum Project (ISCP), a consortium of international schools, developed the PYP and sustained it for over ten years through its collective vision and effort with the goal of producing "a common curriculum framework, for students in the 3–12 age range, which would provide continuity of learning within each school and support the development of international-mindedness on the part of learners" (IBO, n.d.b).

Each of the IB programs includes four foundational and interrelated elements: (1) international mindedness; (2) the IB learner profile; (3) a broad, balanced, conceptual, and connected curriculum; and (4) approaches to teaching and learning (IBO, n.d.b). While the curriculum models for the middle years and diploma programs are interdisciplinary and multidisciplinary, the IB PYP is transdisciplinary. It recognizes how primary-age students learn and "moves learning across, between, and beyond disciplines" (IBO, n.d.b).

Since its introduction, the IB PYP has evolved to become more future-focused in response to the challenges and opportunities within the rapidly changing, complex world, and in line with movements in global education to develop lifelong learners (IBO, n.d.b). The IB PYP curriculum framework emphasizes the central principle of agency that is threaded throughout the three pillars of the curriculum. Through this evolution, the IB PYP provides a framework that is transformational and continues to meet the initial aims of developing internationally minded people who recognize their common humanity and shared guardianship of the planet (IBO, n.d.b). Research finds the following benefits of the IB PYP.

- Standardized test analysis shows that achievement within PYP schools generally exceeds achievement among schools with similar student populations (Gough, Sharpley, Vander Pal, & Griffiths, 2014; Kushner, Cochise, Courtney, Sinnema, & Brown, 2016).

- Research shows positive impacts of the PYP to school climate (Boal & Nakamoto, 2020; Dix & Sniedze-Gregory, 2020).

- PYP students demonstrate consistently higher levels of well-being compared with similar non-PYP students, and PYP schools with strong implementation show higher levels of teacher engagement and student participation (Dix & Sniedze-Gregory, 2020).

Many kinds of schools (state, private, and international) in over 109 countries offer the PYP. As of 2019, a total of 1,782 schools worldwide offered the PYP. Any school educating students ages three to twelve years can apply to implement the PYP and become an IB World School (IBO, n.d.c).

The IBO offers the PYP, Middle Years Programme, Diploma Programme, and its Career-related Programme (introduced in 2014; IBO, n.d.a) to more than 1.95 million students aged three to nineteen across the globe. Schools can offer these IB programs individually or as a continuum of international education. As of February 2022, over 5,400 schools in 159 countries were offering more than 7,500 IB programs. Between 2016 and 2020, the number of IB programs offered worldwide grew by 33.3 percent (IBO, n.d.a). The United States and Canada are the fastest-growing regions for IB, with the total number of IB programs in the United States set to almost double, reaching more than 2,000. In a 2014 report by the IBO, there were 520 candidates for IB World School authorization, and 507 have expressed interest to become IB World School candidates.

PYP in the International School Context

Since 2012, we have had the privilege of visiting and working with high-performing internationally minded schools around the world, including schools that offer the full range of IB programs. Many are considered the top schools in their respective cities and countries, featuring diverse student bodies, lauded teachers, and stunning campuses. While international schools have developed a reputation of being high performing on many levels, a closer look into the culture, mindset, and systems often reveals there are very few systems and structures in place to ensure all students learn at the highest level. In fact, in some instances, underperforming students are systematically coached out of rigorous courses, told to hire external tutors, or even worse, dismissed from their school altogether. Unfortunately, schools labeled *high performing* often receive this badge of honor because of factors unrelated to the levels of learning *all* students obtained.

This shortcoming of international schools led us to implement the Professional Learning Communities (PLC) at Work process to ensure all students achieve at high levels. The research is clear and compelling: implementing the PLC process is the single most effective way to ensure high levels of learning for all students (Stuart et al., 2018). Schools and districts around the world successfully use the process, which is known for supporting schools and districts in raising the achievement and level of learning for underperforming students and students at risk. But what about high-performing schools and schools pushing the pedagogical envelope? Does the PLC process work to improve student learning, when at first glance, learning results may indicate there is nowhere to go but down? Can the PLC process help a school move from good to great even when it appears that things are going well? And most significantly, how can the PLC process work in concert with the IB PYP?

We have found that the PLC process, when well-developed and implemented directly, supports the PYP framework. These two are not separate processes; rather, they are completely intertwined approaches that support a school being both a High Reliability School™ (HRS™) and a highly effective and learning-progressive school. A school can become better when it integrates the PLC process into all aspects of an IB PYP school.

The PLC Process and the PYP

Studies like the one Stuart and colleagues (2018) conducted show PLCs to be effective at raising student achievement in schools around the world, but so far, there has been little examination of how the PLC process works in PYP schools. This may be because of misunderstandings about the PLC process. For example, that the PLC process can only be effective where educators expect strict, empirical outcomes, such as in schools teaching to fixed state or national standards. Certainly, when schools implement a rigid educational model with clear learning expectations, how they implement the PLC process and evaluate its effectiveness are more easily understood. Much has been written to share the research and effectiveness in this context (DuFour, DuFour, Eaker, Many, & Mattos, 2016; DuFour, DuFour, Eaker, Mattos, & Muhammad, 2021). Knowing the effectiveness of PLCs, we as educators and leaders can no longer be put off from implementing the PLC process in schools. Whatever the reason for holding back, clearly the PLC process strongly supports student growth in a wide range of schools—from public to private, urban to rural, and national to international; therefore, leaders in PYP schools should look at how to implement the PLC process in their context.

As practitioners in an international context (outside the lockstep of state or national curricula), where educators are implementing a personalized learning approach, we see the effectiveness of the PLC process outside the traditional environment of a set curriculum. At the same time, we also directly experience how educators can at first struggle to see how the PLC process works in such nontraditional contexts. The PYP is not based on a set of content-based standards, but instead focuses on a concept-driven teaching and learning framework to build up students for future success through a *constructivist approach*—a philosophy, as well as a collection of theories and approaches, with the foundational assumption that knowledge involves constructed supports (Gredler, 2009). All constructivism emphasizes that learners construct meaning in an active, as opposed to passive, way (Oxford, 1997). Both the PLC process and the PYP framework tackle the fundamental question, What do we truly want students to understand, know, and be able to do? (DuFour et al., 2016). This core alignment between the PLC process and PYP framework underlines the compatibility of the two approaches, yet implementing the PLC process in a PYP school is perhaps more complex than in traditional school systems because it requires educators to look at their planning from a new perspective.

High Reliability Schools

In their book *Professional Learning Communities at Work and High Reliability Schools: Cultures of Continuous Learning*, education leaders and researchers Robert Eaker and Robert J. Marzano (2020) present a model based on five hierarchical levels. The HRS model identifies the best practices to implement in schools to raise student achievement and puts forward a clear structure of how educators and leaders can create a school culture and implement structures to ensure all students are safe, healthy, and able to learn at high levels. The HRS model is based on wide-ranging research on issues such as teacher and school leader development, instructional strategies, assessment, and reporting. Eaker and Marzano (2020) identify and explain five levels of performance that define an HRS.

- Level 1: Creating a safe, supportive, and collaborative culture
- Level 2: Developing systems for effective teaching in every classroom
- Level 3: Establishing a guaranteed and viable curriculum
- Level 4: Introducing standards-referenced reporting
- Level 5: Allowing students to personalize through competency-based education

In the HRS model, schools focus their resources to meet the requirements of each level before moving to the next level, eventually attaining level 5, that of an HRS.

In short, the HRS model puts forward an approach that monitors the relationship between actions a school takes and the effectiveness of those actions to produce the desired effects (Marzano, Warrick, Rains, & DuFour, 2018). As schools achieve each HRS level, the model calls on them to be both highly effective and learning progressive. Schools must maintain high levels of learning while ensuring students have time to inquire and be creative in their learning opportunities through their own agency. Around the world, and increasingly within the United States and Canada, schools and districts are adopting the IB PYP as a progressive framework that can provide additional structure and agency to support an HRS, resulting in highly effective, learning-progressive outcomes for students (Stuart et al., 2018).

Eaker and Marzano (2020) outline how the HRS model and the PLC process work hand in hand. In the same way, this book details how the PYP framework and the PLC process are also complementary and work together as tools schools can use to become highly effective, learning-progressive schools.

A highly effective school adheres to the tenets of a PLC and commits to ensuring all students learn at high levels (Stuart et al., 2018). PLCs have systems and structures in place and the mindset necessary for students to succeed in acquiring the knowledge, skills, concepts, and dispositions necessary to thrive in the ever-changing world. In addition, those structures provide students with agency over their own learning, allowing them to personalize their learning and achieve higher levels of learning.

About This Book

This book articulates a clear and compelling case for using the PLC process within the construct of the IB PYP. The contributors to this anthology are elementary school practitioners who have successfully merged the PLC process with the PYP framework. Here, they present the major tenets and intersections between the PLC process, personalized learning, and the PYP. This book explores some of the common themes and challenges facing globally minded, often high-performing schools and how the PLC process can help create a learning-focused culture so schools can ensure *all* students learn and engage at the highest levels. This book will serve as a valuable resource for any school that has adopted the IB PYP and is looking to optimize student learning through a collaborative team model, and for any PLC wishing to adopt the IB PYP.

In chapter 1, "PLC at Work in High-Performing Schools," Timothy S. Stuart provides an overview of the PLC process to give insight into contextualizing PLCs and personalized learning within the IB PYP and how the PLC process and IB PYP combine to create highly effective and learning-progressive schools where all students learn at high levels.

In chapter 2, "PYP and PLC at Work: A Perfect Pair," Kacey Molloy and Rianne Anderson unpack the core components of the PYP framework, beginning with transdisciplinary learning and teaching. They then examine personalization and differentiation within a PYP instructional unit and student agency, connecting these core components to the PLC process.

In chapter 3, "Mathematics and Literacy in the PYP," Yodit Hizekiel provides a detailed explanation for putting the PLC process into practice when teaching mathematics and literacy in a PYP.

In chapter 4, "Response to Intervention in the PYP," Jaqueline Olin discusses the role of response to intervention (RTI) and how the PLC process supports students with special needs in an IB PYP school.

In chapter 5, "Early Years Education and a Pedagogy of *With*," Laura Jo Evans examines what personalized learning can look like in the *early years* (we define as students ages two to five years, or in preschool) within a PLC and PYP context.

In chapter 6, "The Educational Assistant in the PYP and PLC," Eyerusalem Kifle looks at the essential role of educational assistants within the PLC and PYP.

In chapter 7, "Leading Change in the PYP Through PLCs," Calley Connelly examines the role of leaders in the process of learning in an IB PYP school. She provides resources, examples, advice, and specific tools to support the systems, structures, and plans presented in previous chapters as leaders seek to elevate their schools to become highly effective and learning progressive.

Each chapter concludes with a Getting Started on Being Highly Effective section that provides suggested actions for moving toward becoming a highly effective school, as well as a Moving to the Next Level—Becoming Learning Progressive section with suggested actions for becoming a more learning progressive school.

 ## Conclusion

The chapters that follow will walk you through key aspects of implementing the PYP program and how, hand in hand, the PLC process supports that framework to achieve a highly effective, learning-progressive school. The leaders who contributed to this book share their expertise and resources, learned through trial and error, in their own contexts.

In 2021, through the processes laid out in this book, the International Community School (ICS) of Addis Ababa in Ethiopia, where Timothy was head of school and Cal is deputy head of school, became one of only three international schools recognized as an exemplary Model PLC school outside the United States and the first on the African continent. With this book, we hope to pass on the experiences and learning we've gained through our work, as well as our mistakes, with a pathway and essential resources for other schools to help them on their journey.

 # Next Steps

Consider the following suggested actions for getting started on becoming highly effective and then moving to the next level by becoming learning progressive.

Getting Started on Being Highly Effective

- Engage your stakeholders in discussions about where your school wants to be, collect baseline data, and set goals.
- Identify the need and urgency for change with stakeholders.
- Consider having leadership team members engage in professional development to become familiar with the HRS model. We recommend reading *Professional Learning Communities at Work and High Reliability Schools* (Eaker & Marzano, 2020).

Moving to the Next Level—Becoming Learning Progressive

- Consider what structures need to be put in place or improved to allow all students to learn at high levels.
- Develop a culture of continuous improvement within the faculty by aligning the school's pedagogical approach to the school's guiding statements.
- Formalize a process of collecting and reviewing schoolwide student achievement data to inform and monitor school improvement.

References and Resources

Boal, A., & Nakamoto, J. (2020). *School change: How does IB Primary Years Programme implementation impact school climate?* San Francisco: WestEd. Accessed at www.ibo.org/contentassets/af50aa7dc14a4ce4bcc4381dd706c415/pyp -school-change-full-report.pdf on July 26, 2022.

Dix, K., & Sniedze-Gregory, S. (2020). *The impact of the IB Primary Years Programme (PYP) on student wellbeing and other related social-emotional learning outcomes: Report to the International Baccalaureate Organization.* Adelaide, Australia: Australian Council for Educational Research. Accessed at www.ibo.org/globalassets/new-structure/research/pdfs/pyp-wellbeing-full -report-en.pdf on July 26, 2022.

DuFour, R., DuFour, R., Eaker, R., Many, T. W., & Mattos, M. (2016). *Learning by doing: A handbook for Professional Learning Communities at Work* (3rd ed.). Bloomington, IN: Solution Tree Press.

DuFour, R., DuFour, R., Eaker, R., Mattos, M., & Muhammad, A. (2021). *Revisiting Professional Learning Communities at Work: Proven insights for sustained, substantive school improvement* (2nd ed.). Bloomington, IN: Solution Tree Press.

Eaker, R., & Marzano, R. J. (Eds.). (2020). *Professional Learning Communities at Work and High Reliability Schools: Cultures of continuous learning.* Bloomington, IN: Solution Tree Press.

Facer, K. (2021). *Rethinking the "human" at the heart of humanist education.* Accessed at https://en.unesco.org/futuresofeducation/ideas-lab/facer-rethinking -humanist-education on February 28, 2022.

Gredler, M. E. (2009). *Learning and instruction: Theory into practice* (6th ed.). London: Pearson Education.

Gough, A., Sharpley, B., Vander Pal, S., & Griffiths, M. (2014). *The International Baccalaureate Primary Years Programme (PYP) in Victorian Government Primary Schools, Australia: Final report.* Melbourne, Victoria, Australia: RMIT University. Accessed at https://ibo.org/globalassets/new-structure /research/pdfs/pypinaustraliafinalreport.pdf on July 26, 2022.

Hacking, E. B., Blackmore, C., Bullock, K., Bunnell, T., Donnelly, M., & Martin, S. (2017). *The international-mindedness journey: School practices for developing and assessing international-mindedness across the IB continuum.* Accessed at https://ibo.org/globalassets/publications/ib-research/continuum/international-mindedness-summary-2017-en.pdf on May 20, 2022.

International Baccalaureate Organization. (n.d.a). *Facts and figures.* Accessed at www.ibo.org/about-the-ib/facts-and-figures on May 1, 2022.

International Baccalaureate Organization. (n.d.b). *Key facts about the PYP.* Accessed at www.ibo.org/programmes/primary-years-programme/key-facts-about-the-pyp on May 1, 2022.

International Baccalaureate Organization. (n.d.c). *Primary Years Programme.* Accessed at www.ibo.org/programmes/primary-years-programme on April 15, 2022.

International Baccalaureate Organization. (n.d.d). *Our mission.* Accessed at www.ibo.org/about-the-ib/mission on May 20, 2022.

International Baccalaureate Organization. (2014). *A dynamic presence: Growth and characteristics of IB world schools.* Accessed at www.dcds.edu/uploaded/Buzz/December_2014/UnitedStatesCountryProfile.pdf on July 24, 2020.

International Baccalaureate Organization. (2018). *Learning and teaching in the enhanced PYP.* Accessed at https://blogs.ibo.org/sharingpyp/files/2018/02/2018-January-Learning-teaching-part-1-ENG.pdf on April 15, 2022.

International Baccalaureate Organization. (2020). *Key findings from research on the Primary Years Programme.* Accessed at www.ibo.org/globalassets/new-structure/research/pdfs/research-pyp-key-findings-en.pdf on July 26, 2022.

Kushner, S., Cochise, A., Courtney, M., Sinnema, C., & Brown, G. (2016). *International Baccalaureate Primary Years Programme in Aotearoa New Zealand: A case study in whole-school innovation.* Bethesda, MD: International Baccalaureate Organization.

Marzano, R. J., Norford, J. S., Finn, M., & Finn, D, III. (2017). *A handbook for personalized competency-based education.* Bloomington, IN: Marzano Resources.

Marzano, R. J., Warrick, P. B., Rains, C. L., & DuFour, R. (2018). *Leading a High Reliability School.* Bloomington, IN: Solution Tree Press.

Oxford, R. L. (1997). Constructivism: Shape-shifting, substance, and teacher education application. *Peabody Journal of Education, 72*(1), 35–66.

Stuart, T. S., Heckmann, S., Mattos, M., & Buffum, A. (2018). *Personalized learning in a PLC at Work: Student agency through the four critical questions.* Bloomington, IN: Solution Tree Press.

CHAPTER 1

PLC at Work in High-Performing Schools

Timothy S. Stuart

Moving from a teaching-focused school to a learning-focused school is a challenging undertaking. It is even more challenging if the teaching and learning are already above average, such as in high-performing schools. The promise of increased learning is less compelling if student learning targets are already being met. There is little sense of urgency, and the fear of disrupting—or even destroying—the magic that is already happening in these schools academically can be a significant inhibitor of change.

For many high-performing schools, a more compelling argument takes shape about the quest for continuous improvement and professional growth. The opportunity to learn from and with the outstanding educator next door is huge. For teachers in high-performing schools, the single biggest benefit of the professional learning community (PLC) process is the unmatched professional growth that comes with becoming vulnerable enough with colleagues to be willing to challenge every teaching strategy, assessment item, and intervention method to better serve students.

At a schoolwide level, PLCs create the infrastructure to deliver on the promises we make to our community members: the ability to guarantee that we will do everything in our power to ensure every student learns the intended curriculum, is assessed in a fair and consistent manner, and receives timely, formative feedback and interventions when needed.

One of the advantages of schools that have embraced or are in the process of moving toward an International Baccalaureate (IB) curriculum is that they can attract top-tier, highly qualified, and experienced teachers from around the world who bring their worldviews and diverse pedagogical approaches to the classroom. All these factors can create a beautifully diverse and high-performing culture that can have a positive impact on a school's culture. However, this collection of highly independent teachers can also lead to inconsistency in instructional and assessment practices. The quality of instruction, feedback, and interventions can depend entirely on the teacher a student happens to be assigned to, which is contrary to the concept of a guaranteed curriculum.

What follows is a brief overview of the PLC process. This is not intended to be a comprehensive treatise on PLCs as there are entire books on the topic, but rather to give insight into how to contextualize PLCs and personalized learning within the PYP context. As an international educator who has served in high-performing schools on four continents, I am more convinced than ever that PLCs are the single most powerful way to maximize learning for all students. Nothing else even comes close.

What Is a PLC?

PLC at Work process architects Richard DuFour and Robert Eaker, along with experts Rebecca DuFour, Thomas W. Many, and Mike Mattos, define PLCs as "an ongoing process in which educators work collaboratively in recurring cycles of collective inquiry and action research in order to achieve better results for the students they serve" (DuFour, DuFour, Eaker, Many, & Mattos, 2016, p. 10). On a macro-level, the entire school is a PLC with specific systems and structures in place that allow all teachers to collaborate with other professionals to give students the opportunity to achieve at high levels. On a micro-level, PLCs are made up of collaborative teams of teachers who meet regularly to engage in learning-focused conversations designed to improve instructional practice and impact student learning.

There are a variety of ways schools can construct collaborative teams within a PLC at Work, the most common being teams of teachers who teach the same course or the same grade level. While some schools are large and have several teachers instructing a common course or grade level, some schools may only have one teacher per course or grade level. These schools must find creative ways to form teams of teachers with similar learning targets for their students. In short, high-performing collaborative teams are most effective when they have the same answer to the first of four PLC critical questions: What do we want students to know, understand, and be able to do? (DuFour et al., 2016). Identifying common learning targets when teaching different courses is most easily accomplished when the learning target is elevated beyond discipline-specific content to transdisciplinary concepts, transdisciplinary skills, or even learning dispositions. In fact, these concepts, skills, and dispositions are what students should be learning in the first place.

The PLC process impacts student learning by ensuring teachers stay focused on what matters most: learning. The process prevents a collaborative team from becoming a gathering of teachers who work on a common task or study a book together, but never intentionally consider student learning.

The PLC process is organized on three big ideas: (1) a focus on learning, (2) a collaborative culture and collective responsibility, and (3) a focus on results (DuFour et al., 2016).

A Focus on Learning

The first big idea of a PLC is a focus on learning (DuFour et al., 2016). This may sound obvious and simplistic, but many schools focus on teaching more than on learning. High-performing schools boast the ability to hire some of the best teachers in the world. While this is certainly a huge asset, it does come with a price. Great teachers often receive accolades because they are fun to work with, are the toughest teachers in the school, give the most amount of homework, or are the hardest graders. But sadly, schools rarely measure teachers by how much their students learn. Moving a school from being teaching focused to being learning focused is one of the first steps necessary to create a PLC culture.

A Collaborative Culture and Collective Responsibility

The second big idea of a PLC is a collaborative culture and collective responsibility (DuFour et al., 2016). In his book *Creating Innovators*, Tony Wagner (2012), senior research fellow at the Learning Policy Institute, suggests there is no innovation without collaboration; it is very difficult to generate new ideas working alone. This is true for teachers. When teachers work collaboratively to examine student results, they can collectively identify the best approach to teaching. When teachers work together, they learn together, teacher practice improves, and student learning increases. It's simple, but teachers in high-performing schools are often hired because of their independent, nonconformist spirit. They may be teachers administrators consider experts in their fields and who do not require a whole lot of structure and supervision to get the job done. The question is, have even *these* teachers, with their everyday magic, placed a ceiling on their growth and innovation at a certain point by going it alone?

In PLCs, collaborative teams take collective responsibility for the learning of their students (DuFour et al., 2016). *Collective responsibility* implies being mutually accountable for their work. Collaborative team members hold one another accountable to teach the agreed-on curriculum, use team-developed common formative assessments, and reach the established learning goals. In high-performing PLCs, *my* students become *our* students. Taking collective responsibility allows teams to maximize the strengths of the individuals to ensure high levels of learning for *all* students.

A Focus on Results

The third big idea of a PLC is a focus on results—teams assess their effectiveness based on student results, not intentions (DuFour et al., 2016). There are many school parking lots paved with good intentions (DuFour, 2018). High-performing schools are no different. Because there are sometimes few external measurements holding these schools accountable for learning outcomes—and one could argue that many students in these schools will do relatively well regardless of how they are taught—it is easy to believe that great teaching is synonymous with great learning. Some schools fall into the trap of assuming that by hiring some of the most knowledgeable, experienced, engaging, and passionate teachers, students are learning at high levels. But are they? What's the evidence? A commitment to the PLC process requires a commitment to monitoring student learning results.

What Do PLCs Do?

PLCs provide teachers with the time and structure to grow professionally by answering the four critical questions of learning (DuFour et al., 2016). These questions may seem simple, and they are, but they have proven to have a significant impact on student learning when a team of teachers asks and answers them regularly:

1. What knowledge, skills, and dispositions should every student acquire as a result of this unit, this course, or this grade level?
2. How will we know when each student has acquired the essential knowledge and skills?
3. How will we respond when some students do not learn?
4. How will we extend the learning for students who are already proficient? (DuFour et al., 2016, p. 36)

These four PLC critical questions serve as the basis for the action research collaborative teams conduct. The answers to these simple questions allow collaborative teams to articulate clear, consistent, and obtainable learning targets; develop common formative assessments that align to these targets; and develop interventions and extensions for students who may need additional support or the opportunity to go beyond the articulated curriculum. Yes, it's that simple. When teachers ask and act on these questions, students learn more.

I have heard schools talk about "doing PLCs." When asked to explain what they actually do in a PLC, their answers often refer to doing clerical work as a department, planning lessons, studying a book together with other teachers, or identifying a personal and professional goal with colleagues and holding one another accountable to that goal. These are all wonderful activities and certainly have a place in schools, but a school is not a PLC if teachers are not regularly and systematically answering the four critical questions of learning within their collaborative teams.

What Is a Highly Effective and Learning-Progressive School?

A highly effective school is a school that adheres to the tenets of a PLC and commits to ensuring all students learn at high levels (Stuart, Heckmann, Mattos, & Buffum, 2018). These PLCs have all the systems and structures in place and the mindset necessary for students to succeed in the acquisition of the knowledge, skills, concepts, and dispositions necessary to thrive in this ever-changing world.

A highly effective and learning-progressive school adds one important construct to the mix: student agency. Giving students agency over their own learning allows them to personalize their learning and achieve higher levels of learning. It's one thing to be a school where the adults have clarity about the desired learning targets, assessments that align to those learning targets, appropriate interventions for students who are not learning, and extension opportunities for students who demonstrate mastery of those learning targets. It's another thing altogether when teachers give students the opportunity to own their learning by asking and answering the same critical questions: (1) What is it that I want to know, understand, and be able to do? (2) How will I demonstrate that I know it? (3) What will I do when I am not learning? and (4) What will I do when I already know it (Stuart et al., 2018)?

Conclusion

The PLC at Work process continues to prove itself as the most powerful and effective collaborative school framework. When implemented faithfully, the process ensures all students learn at the highest levels when teams of teachers ask and answer the four critical questions. It also provides a framework that allows students to engage in their own learning process by asking and answering the four critical questions for themselves. The PLC at Work process is therefore the ideal framework to support the transdisciplinary and agentic learning at the core of the IB PYP. Subsequent chapters explore the intersection of the PLC process, personalized learning with student agency, and the IB PYP. I believe all these constructs can help a school move toward its goal of becoming a highly effective and learning-progressive school.

Next Steps

Consider the following suggested actions for getting started on becoming highly effective and then moving to the next level by becoming learning progressive.

Getting Started on Being Highly Effective

- Commit to becoming a highly effective school by putting systems in place to ensure all students learn at the highest levels.
- Consider attending a PLC at Work Institute near you (www .solutiontree.com/events.html).
- Create a *guiding coalition* (or school leadership team) to help all staff learn the PLC implementation process.
- Create time for teachers to collaborate and have learning-focused conversations.
- Ensure collaborative teams are asking and answering the four critical questions of a PLC.

Moving to the Next Level—Becoming Learning Progressive

- Commit to becoming a learning-progressive school by empowering students to own their learning.

- Consider reading *Personalized Learning in a PLC at Work* (Stuart et al., 2018).

- Find ways to give students agency over their learning by asking and answering the four critical questions for themselves.

 # References and Resources

DuFour, R. (2018). *Passion & persistence* [Video file]. Bloomington, IN: Solution Tree Press.

DuFour, R., DuFour, R., Eaker, R., Many, T. W., & Mattos, M. (2016). *Learning by doing: A handbook for Professional Learning Communities at Work* (3rd ed.). Bloomington, IN: Solution Tree Press.

Stuart, T. S., Heckmann, S., Mattos, M., & Buffum, A. (2018). *Personalized learning in a PLC at Work: Student agency through the four critical questions.* Bloomington, IN: Solution Tree Press.

Wagner, T. (2012). *Creating innovators: The making of young people who will change the world.* New York: Scribner.

Kacey Molloy is a Primary Years Programme (PYP) coordinator at the International Community School (ICS) of Addis Ababa in Ethiopia. Formerly an elementary classroom teacher, she is passionate about creating engaging, meaningful experiences for children to construct understanding and develop their thinking skills. Kacey has worked in schools in Ethiopia, Bangladesh, North Macedonia, and the United States (Montana). She served as a Peace Corps volunteer early in her career and worked with teachers on capacity development. In 2022, Kacey continued her professional journey by moving into the role of assistant principal of elementary at the International School of Kenya.

Kacey received a bachelor's degree in elementary education from the University of Montana and a master's degree in education from State University of New York College at Buffalo. She is pursuing a doctorate in educational leadership at East Carolina University.

Rianne Anderson is a passionate elementary educator and curriculum coordinator. She began her teaching career in 2006 as a lower elementary teacher in her home state of Colorado. Her passion and drive as a lifelong learner, coach, and facilitator led her into positions of leadership. She has taught and led in multiple schools in Colorado and at the International Community School (ICS) of Addis Ababa in Ethiopia. Rianne has extensive experience with the International Baccalaureate Primary Years Programme (IBP PYP) and roots her practice in inquiry and conceptual understanding. She seeks out opportunities for meaningful collaboration to support and extend adult and student learning.

Throughout her career, Rianne has engaged in a variety of professional learning opportunities related to the written, taught, and assessed curriculum; the role of leaders; and implementing change in education. She is coauthor of a blog on strategies to build an inquiry-driven community.

Rianne received a bachelor's degree in human development and family studies with an endorsement in early childhood education at Colorado State University. She earned a master's degree in education at Lesley University in Cambridge, Massachusetts.

To book Kacey Molloy or Rianne Anderson for professional development, contact pd@SolutionTree.com.

CHAPTER 2

PYP and PLC at Work: A Perfect Pair

Kacey Molloy and Rianne Anderson

The International Baccalaureate Primary Years Programme (IB PYP) is a curriculum framework that centers on an inquiry approach and aims for conceptual understandings. Highlighting a student-centered approach and promoting student agency, the PYP provides a framework for the development of concept-based, transdisciplinary units of study. The development of the whole student is a driving belief of the PYP. Educators consider knowledge, while valued, as only one piece of the complex puzzle; dispositions (learner profile traits), conceptual understandings, and transdisciplinary skills (approaches to learning) hold considerable importance. The IB PYP aims to develop globally minded citizens who can flourish in an ever-changing world (International Baccalaureate Organization [IBO], 2022).

Professional Learning Communities at Work (PLCs; DuFour, DuFour, Eaker, Many, & Mattos, 2016) are schools in which teams of teachers meet regularly to collaborate to achieve better learning results for students and improve teaching. Four critical questions provide the process to guide collaborative, data-informed conversations in teacher teams (DuFour et al., 2016). Data are a driving force in PLCs; valid data allow teachers to undertake collaboration with fidelity.

Upon initial examination of the PLC process and the IB PYP framework, it may be difficult to see how they fit together; they almost seem like juxtapositions, at odds with each other when considering their philosophical ideals. How can educators follow the lead of their students, encouraging agency and inquiry, when the focus on data and numbers is at the center of the conversations? Which is more important when making educational decisions: student understanding of concepts or the mastery of skills? In trying to implement both the IB PYP framework and the PLC process, one can feel much like a NASA scientist helping *Apollo 13* return safely to Earth or trying to fit a square peg into a round hole.

You may be reading this book having had experience with either PLCs or the IB PYP. If you are a skilled PLC collaborator, you may feel the data and numbers are the most important part of the conversation. On the other hand, if you are coming from an IB PYP background, you may believe student questions, inquiries, and understanding of concepts should hold more importance. Throughout this chapter, our goal is to help you realize that the IB PYP framework and PLC process work together to improve student learning. When striving to become a highly effective, learning-progressive school, these two models complement each other to deepen and extend student learning (Stuart, Heckmann, Mattos, & Buffum, 2018).

To begin to grasp how the IB PYP framework and PLC process can work together, it is imperative to unpack the core components of the IB PYP framework, beginning with transdisciplinary learning and teaching.

What Is Transdisciplinary Learning?

Imagine this: you look out your window and notice your yard needs work. You are envious of your neighbors who have spaces conducive to parties and quiet reflection over a cup of tea. You have the time, resources, and motivation to give your yard a facelift, yet you are not quite sure where to start. From previous experience, you know conducting a quick search online will most likely result in inspirational photos showing potential opportunities. You hop online and enter *outdoor spaces* into the search engine. Up pops a plethora of beautiful, inviting photos that immediately open your mind to a world of possibilities. A quick scroll through the photos has you noting elements that are aesthetically pleasing. These include types of seating arrangements, materials, color schemes, flora and fauna, lighting, and furniture styles.

Your head swarming with ideas, you bring yourself back to the reality of your budget, time, and space. This helps you home in on your priorities. You grab a pad of paper and pencil to begin sketching your ideas. You know your space only allows for a small seating area if you want room for greenery, so you take that into account when creating your sketch. Equipped with this initial thinking, you head to your local garden shop to see what you can purchase within your budget. Perhaps you are even a crafting expert and can use your do-it-yourself skills to get the most out of your budget. Over time, you acquire the pieces of furniture, textiles, and lighting to actualize your vision.

Concurrently, you research plants to determine what will thrive in your environment. Asking experts and referencing texts such as blog posts, books, and gardening magazines helps equip you with the knowledge and understanding you need to select the right flowers and shrubbery. The result of all your hard work is a beautiful space you designed from start to finish. You eagerly invite others over to enjoy your new garden.

Now, take a step outside that story and consider what understandings, knowledge, skills, and dispositions you employed to imagine, design, and actualize your garden space. You engaged understandings in various disciplines.

- **Mathematics:** Spatial awareness, geometry, money, and measurement

- **Literacy:** Reading and synthesizing information

- **Science:** Understanding climate and the earth cycles (especially regarding plants and choice in materials)

- **Social studies:** Economic and personal decision making

You also had to employ multiple skills that transcend disciplines.

- **Research skills:** Source selection and gathering and synthesizing information

- **Thinking skills:** Creative thinking as you designed the space and critical thinking in determining what would and would not belong

- **Self-management:** Managing time and resources

As this example demonstrates, a person must employ knowledge, skills, understandings, and dispositions when approaching and resolving a problem; disciplines are not siloed in life, and they should not be siloed in school either. The IB PYP recognizes this fact and emphasizes real-life, authentic learning. Certainly, developing discipline-specific skills is necessary to be successful, however, we do students a disservice by developing these skills in isolation without also intentionally helping students make connections to how they can utilize these skills in other contexts. It is imperative for educators to help students connect learning across disciplines. The driving IB PYP document *Learning and Teaching* (IBO, 2018b) states:

> Transdisciplinarity transgresses subjects. It begins and ends with a problem, an issue, or a theme. Students' interests and questions form the heart of transdisciplinary learning. It is a curriculum-organizing approach where human commonalities rise to the top without regard for subject boundaries. Subjects become an instrument/tool/resource to explore a theme, problem, or concept in depth. The result is a different or new organizing framework. (p. 2)

The garden design example illustrates an in-depth exploration of a problem. It demonstrates evidence of the transfer of learning to new contexts. The IB PYP framework aims to do the same. Teachers intentionally design transdisciplinary units of inquiry, cornerstone pieces of the framework, to ensure these opportunities for connections arise.

What Are the Core Components of a Transdisciplinary Unit of Inquiry?

A *unit of inquiry* encompasses conceptual understandings, knowledge, skills, and dispositions. Within a transdisciplinary unit of inquiry, these essential elements include subject-specific learning targets, and aim to develop transferable skills and understandings. The garden example illustrates how fluidly people employ knowledge, skills, and understandings in life, and the aim of a transdisciplinary unit of inquiry is to provide contexts that encourage students to do the same. The power of the PYP is that it provides a framework for creating these units.

In the PYP framework, teachers organize a transdisciplinary unit of inquiry into one of six themes. These themes highlight the shared human experience, have global significance, and provide students with the opportunity to construct understanding through rich, meaningful, collaborative engagement. The themes provide a balanced structure to the overall program while also offering flexibility to inquire into various contexts and interests (IBO, 2018a). The IB PYP provides detailed descriptors that break down each theme and provide more context through which to develop a unit of inquiry. The theme descriptors are as follows (IBO, 2018b). We have found units to be stronger when narrowing in on particular descriptor lines within a theme as opposed to the theme in general. This creates more specificity and builds a strong program of inquiry across the school.

- **Who we are:** An inquiry into . . .
  + The nature of the self
  + Beliefs and values
  + Personal, physical, mental, social, and spiritual health
  + Human relationships, including families, friends, communities, and cultures
  + Rights and responsibilities
  + What it means to be human

- **Where we are in place and time:** An inquiry into . . .

    + Orientation in place and time

    + Personal histories, homes, and journeys

    + The discoveries, explorations, and migrations of humankind

    + The relationships between, and the interconnectedness of, individuals and civilizations, from local and global perspectives

- **How we express ourselves:** An inquiry into . . .

    + The ways in which we discover and express ideas, feelings, nature, culture, beliefs, and values

    + The ways in which we reflect on, extend, and enjoy our creativity

    + Our appreciation of the aesthetic

- **How the world works:** An inquiry into . . .

    + The natural world and its laws

    + The interaction between the natural world (physical and biological) and human societies

    + How humans use their understanding of scientific principles

    + The impact of scientific and technological advances on society and on the environment

- **How we organize ourselves:** An inquiry into . . .

    + The interconnectedness of human-made systems and communities

    + The structure and function of organizations

    + Societal decision making

    + Economic activities and their impact on humankind and the environment

- **Sharing the planet:** An inquiry into . . .

    + Rights and responsibilities in the struggle to share finite resources with other people and with other living things

    + Communities and the relationships within and between them

    + Access to equal opportunities

    + Peace and conflict resolution (IBO, 2018b, p. 11)

It is essential that teams begin their collaborative work by coming to a common understanding of the theme and the part of the theme descriptor driving the unit. It is not merely enough to agree; the team must engage in discussion about the theme and its description so members begin their work with complete clarity on the basis for the unit. The team uses this clarity to determine the other essential elements of the unit.

Within the identified theme, the unit of inquiry contains specific elements that provide depth and breadth. Teams initially select or craft these essential elements. They include the central idea (the enduring understanding), lines of inquiry, key concepts, related concepts, approaches to learning skills, and learner profile traits (see figure 2.1).

Key Concepts	Transdisciplinary Theme	Approaches to Learning
Function Connection Perspective	An inquiry into the ways in which we discover and express ideas, feelings, nature, culture, beliefs, and values; the ways in which we reflect on, extend, and enjoy our creativity; our appreciation of the aesthetic	Communication skills • Listening • Interpreting • Speaking • Writing • Reading
	Central Idea **People express their ideas through different forms of storytelling.**	
Related Concepts		**Learner Profile**
Expression Imagination Structure Form Change (art)	**Lines of Inquiry** • How storytelling works (function) • How people connect with each other through stories (connection) • The ways in which stories can be expressed and interpreted (perspective)	Communicator Open-minded

FIGURE 2.1: Sample grade 2 transdisciplinary unit of inquiry.

Unpacking the theme to reach clarity and then working together to put the essential pieces together take devoted attention. Collaborative time is essential to the process. If possible, we suggest setting aside several hours to engage in a *planning retreat*—a dedicated, focused meeting to design or unpack a unit of inquiry. Even entering an already well-designed unit necessitates time to unpack, especially if team members are new. Planning retreats that include all members of the teaching team (including collaborating single-subject teachers) can lead to much stronger implementation, allowing all members to be clear about the learning intentions. While reaching this point in the unit design process is important, it does not fully answer PLC critical question one, What do we want students to know, understand, and be able to do? In the next section, we help to bring to the forefront a level of specificity in answering this question that is often unreached in IB PYP schools.

What Do We Want Students to Know, Understand, and Be Able to Do?

The success of a unit rides on the clear and specific answer to PLC critical question one. The essential elements of the IB we outlined previously are critical to the formation of a unit of inquiry; however, teams often make the mistake of stopping there when engaging in conversations aimed at designing or unpacking the unit. They quickly proceed to discussions about success criteria or even the planning of learning engagements. The problem with jumping into conversations of what the unit might look like too quickly is that a critical piece has been left out: *articulation of what students should know, understand, and be able to do*—the first critical question of a PLC (DuFour et al., 2016). A common misconception exists that the unit essentials are the answer to critical question one, but take a moment to consider if this is true. Use the example in figure 2.1. Would you have complete clarity about expectations for students by the end of the unit regarding their conceptual understanding, knowledge, skills, and development of dispositions? If you examined these essentials with a teaching partner, would your partner share the same expectations? Stopping the unit-unpacking conversation after the completion of the essential unit elements (as figure 2.1 shows) results in a lack of clear understanding of the learning goals for the unit. It is critical that collaborative teams spend time articulating with clarity what they want students to know, understand, and be able to do (PLC critical question one) by the end of the unit. The discussion about critical question one must get to a granular level to ensure all members of the collaborative team share a complete understanding of the learning goals.

The PYP has always identified the importance of articulating the answer to PLC critical question one, as demonstrated through the learning goals and success criteria planning stage (see figure 2.2, page 28). The first half of this stage, *learning goals*, addresses the answer to PLC critical question one. The second half, *success criteria*, addresses the answer to PLC critical question two, which we discuss at length next in this chapter. Although updates in requirements provide PYP schools with more agency in their planning process (IBO, 2018a), outlining the learning goals and success criteria remains a fundamental part of the planning process.

PLC Critical Question One: What do we want students to know, understand, and be able to do?		Unit: Grade:
Central Idea: **Lines of Inquiry:**		
Key Concepts:		Related Concepts:
Students will understand . . . • • •		
Know—Knowledge required to access the central idea	Do—Skills required for information literacy	Be—Dispositions required in the learner's profile
Students will know . . . • • •	Students will be able to . . . • • •	Students will be . . . • • •

Source: © 2021 by International Community School of Addis Ababa. Adapted with permission.

FIGURE 2.2: Template for PLC critical question one—What do we want students to know, understand, and be able to do?

*Visit **go.SolutionTree.com/PLCbooks** for a free reproducible version of this figure.*

Collaboratively identifying the essential elements of the unit, along with clearly articulating the answer to PLC critical question one, is vital to ensure collective understanding of the learning goals. These learning goals are often dependent on the school and its adopted scope-and-sequence documents. Some schools may use national standards, others may follow the IB PYP published scope-and-sequence documents, and still others may use a combination (IBO, 2018a). Often, national standards focus narrowly on content knowledge and skills; due to the conceptual nature of the PYP, it is imperative that teams also identify driving conceptual understandings and dispositions. Taking time to understand how knowledge, skills, and dispositions work in service of conceptual understandings is a key piece to fully articulate the answer to PLC critical question one.

How Will We Know If They Learned It?

With solid understanding and documentation of the answer to the first PLC critical question, it is time to move on to critical question two: How will we know if they learned it? (DuFour et al., 2016). As demonstrated in the discussion of the first PLC critical question, the IB PYP planning process aligns with the PLC process in asking and answering the four critical questions. The IB articulates this itself, although not directly citing DuFour and colleagues (2016) or PLCs (IBO, 2018b). Instead, the answer to critical question two typically comes in the form of *success criteria*. To determine the answer to critical question two, educators should ask themselves, "What success criteria will we use to determine the level of a student's depth of understanding?" Determining the answer to this question before the unit begins is vital; teams will use these criteria throughout the unit when examining student evidence, which teams use to inform how the unit unfolds.

IB PYP teachers may find themselves struggling to effectively answer the second critical question, especially when considering how to evaluate understandings and dispositions. Educators can more easily assess knowledge and skills through checklists, but what about understandings? This is where careful selection of an assessment tool comes into play. Models such as the SOLO (structure of observed learning outcomes) Taxonomy (Biggs, n.d.; Biggs & Collis, 1982), single-point rubrics, or conceptually designed analytic rubrics are examples of tools that support answering PLC critical question two within a conceptually focused unit of inquiry. Likewise, careful consideration of tools to support the assessment of growth in identified dispositions is important. When assessing growth in dispositions, continuums play a vital role.

Many considerations come into play when deciding which tool is best for your team and group of learners. Students' age and developmental readiness and educators' experience should be considerations when determining which tool will best support learning and teaching. Taking this another step, the IB PYP highly encourages co-construction of the tool to honor and embed student voice and to facilitate a deeper understanding of the learning goals. In fact, *agency*, or voice, choice, and ownership, is a grounding belief of the IB PYP, which we discuss in more detail later in this chapter.

Figure 2.3 (page 30) is an example of a conceptually designed SOLO Taxonomy, adapted from Michael Hughes, an educator at Seisen International School.

Grade 1: Sharing the Planet

Central Idea: Living things have unique characteristics that help them survive in a shared habitat.

Understandings Assessed	No Current Understanding	Surface Understanding		Deeper Understanding	
		Learning outcomes at these levels are designed to allow students to gather ideas and information. They are knowledge based and driven by the essential knowledge the curriculum identifies to support conceptual understanding.		Learning outcomes at these levels require the students to think deeper. They use the ideas and knowledge gained in the previous levels to make connections, conceptualize, and transfer their understanding.	
	Prestructural (I need help to generate an idea.)	Unistructural (I have one idea.)	Multistructural (I have many ideas.)	Relational (I can connect my ideas.)	Extended Abstract (I can take my ideas further.)
	Getting Started	Investigating		Connecting Ideas	Going Further
Line of inquiry: The characteristics of living things **Conceptual understandings:** Everything has unique, identifiable *characteristics.* (Form, classification)	I need help getting started.	I can *identify* a characteristic of a living thing.	I can *identify* many characteristics of living things.	I *classify* living things upon their characteristics.	I can *transfer* my understanding of characteristics to other areas. (For example, shapes in mathematics, text features, and music genres.)

				I transfer my understanding of form and function to other areas. (For example, we have quiet spaces or caves in our hubs due to the busyness of the space.)
Line of inquiry: How unique characteristics help living things survive in their environment (Conditions) **Conceptual understandings:** *Characteristics function to help living things survive in their shared habitat.* (Function) (The focus is on the *conditions* of the habitat in relation to form and survival.)	I need help getting started.	I can identify *one function of a characteristic* that helps a living thing survive in the *conditions* of its habitat.	I can identify *functions of many characteristics* that help living things survive in the *conditions* of their habitats.	*I connect my understanding of characteristics and habitat conditions* by explaining shared characteristics of a habitat. (For example, many animals in the Arctic have thick fur or blubber due to the cold conditions; many living things in deserts have the ability to store water.)
Line of inquiry: How unique characteristics help living things survive alongside others **Conceptual understandings:** *Characteristics function to help living things survive in their shared habitat.* (Function) (The focus is on the *other living things* in the habitat in relation to form and survival.)	I need help getting started.	I can identify *one function of a characteristic* that helps a living thing survive *alongside others* in a habitat.	I can identify *functions of many characteristics* that help living things survive *alongside others* in a habitat.	*I connect my understanding of characteristics and other living things in a habitat* by exploring shared characteristics.

Source: © *2021 by Michael Hughes, Seisen International School, Tokyo. Adapted with permission.*

FIGURE 2.3: Grade 1 sharing the planet SOLO Taxonomy.

What Are *Data*?

To have meaningful, rich discussions about PLC critical question two, it is necessary to unpack the term *data*. What do educators mean when they discuss data? Often the preconceived notion is that *data* mean numbers. For example, educators can gather data (numbers) specific to student reading levels and mathematics fluency. They can engage in meaningful conversations utilizing the four critical questions and make educational decisions for how to support students who demonstrate they have not mastered the intended learning (question three), as well as next steps for the students who demonstrate they already know it (question four). While this understanding of PLCs and data is most certainly meaningful, it leaves some questions unanswered. For instance, how can you engage in rich conversations about the four critical questions when the intended understanding is not quantifiable with a number? Proper inquiry is difficult to represent with a number. Assessing conceptual understanding is not the same as assessing a reading level. There are no formal assessments to gather data on the approaches to learning skills (ATLs), five categories of skills that transcend subject boundaries, or the learner profile, attributes educators deem important for internationally minded citizens and change makers (IBO, 2018a). Therefore, is it possible to engage in the PLC process in these areas?

It is necessary to realize that data are not synonymous with numbers; they're much more complex. *Data* refer to facts or information. In the struggle to understand data-driven dialogue, it is imperative to not underestimate the role of qualitative data. Data are the evidence teachers and students collect every day that demonstrates where students are in their learning. Data can look like numbers, but they can also look like information regarding students' interests, ideas, and misconceptions. Data may come from conversations overheard or the way a student approaches a problem. In fact, it's even possible to quantify qualitative data using tools such as rubrics and continuums. Data are accessible to educators in almost every moment of time with students—educators just must document them.

To gather these types of data, you must become inquirers into your students. You should lean in and listen to students' questions and conversations. You should consider more than just subject-specific skills and knowledge; also consider who your students are as individuals. This includes their assets regarding matters such as interests, dispositions, and transdisciplinary skills. The realization that every moment of the day provides an opportunity to gather data and analyze those data to determine the next steps (PLC critical questions three and four) opens a new page on the PLC and IB PYP journey. This understanding helps exemplify how the IB PYP framework and PLC process can fit together and complement each other.

Once a collaborative team has fully articulated and come to a common understanding of the answers to PLC critical questions one and two, the unit can begin. This is when the student inquiry starts. Although the unit has clear learning goals and success criteria, the method of reaching those goals will be different for each individual student or group of students. The learning journey will take a personalized path based on students' interests and background knowledge. This is where the power of PLC critical questions three and four comes into play. These questions allow educators to meet students where they are and nudge them forward on their own personal learning journey. In some cases, educators will determine a response for the students who are demonstrating that they are stuck (question three) and for other students, extending and going deeper when they demonstrate proficiency in the identified knowledge, skills, and understandings (question four). When a collaborative team meets to discuss questions three and four, it is necessary to bring student data. What are students showing they know, understand, and can do? What misconceptions are students displaying? What new theories are emerging from students? What new interests are students revealing? Based on the answers to these questions, educators can decide how to respond in real time to ensure all students reach the team-outlined learning goals in response to PLC critical question one.

Utilizing a virtual mind map tool, such as Coggle (https://coggle.it), is helpful when documenting collaborative conversations regarding PLC critical questions three and four. This type of tool allows educators to collaboratively map out the learning story and document different paths for different groups of students.

In the previous sections, we provided guidance about asking and answering the four PLC critical questions through a teacher-driven lens, but it is possible to take a learner-centered approach, and we encourage you to consider what this might look like. How can you involve students in determining what they need and how they might move forward? This is where agency comes into play.

What Is Agency?

If the PYP outlines the critical role agency plays within the learning process (IBO, 2018a), you may ask, "Where is agency if the success criteria are already determined?" The answer to this query lies in the ways students choose to demonstrate their learning. Supporting and encouraging learners to demonstrate their understanding using a method of their choosing align with the foundational beliefs of the IB PYP. But this is only part of the assessment process. The PLC process asks educators to use their chosen assessment tool to analyze students' depth of understanding. This analysis is an ongoing process throughout a unit of inquiry as it informs discussions about PLC critical questions three and four and helps in determining next steps.

Asking and answering critical questions three and four provide opportunities for educators to differentiate a unit based on individual student needs. While mostly teacher driven, this form of differentiation is certainly important to meet students where they are. The next level, however, is personalization. *Personalization* is a student-driven approach to differentiation. Facilitating a culture where students begin to ask and answer the four critical questions takes student understanding of their own learning to the next level (Stuart et al., 2018). When students can articulate their answers to the four questions, they will have more ownership of their learning. As educators strive to teach students how to learn, the critical questions provide a structure for students that encourages them to pursue areas of interest. As students ask themselves, "What is it I want to know, understand, and be able to do?" "How will I know if I've learned it?" "What will I do if I'm stuck?" and "What will I do if I already know it?" they begin to understand the learning process more deeply and how to help themselves (Stuart et al., 2018).

This personalized approach to the learning process, while exciting, is certainly challenging when thinking of logistics and developmental readiness. The younger students are, the more scaffolding they may need. The *PYP exhibition*, "the culminating, collaborative experience in the final year of the PYP," is a perfect fit for this approach (IBO, 2018c, p. 40). As you consider how this might look in younger students, we urge you to consider trying it out on a much smaller scale. You may consider providing opportunities for students to begin asking and answering one of the critical questions. For example, engaging students in a rich dialogue about critical question three, "What will I do if I don't know it?" provides an opportunity for students to examine "the learning pit"—being "stuck in the learning" where "making mistakes, failing, and not knowing are essential parts of the learning journey" (Stonefield Schools, 2022)—and ways that they might advocate for their own learning needs.

Additionally, exploring ways of demonstrating understanding (critical question two), as suggested previously, provides students with the agency to determine how they might communicate and display their knowledge, skills, dispositions, and understandings in real-world settings. By providing opportunities for students to engage in these rich conversations about their own learning, educators are developing a culture of thinking and understanding of the learning process. What could be more valuable than students having a deep understanding of their own learning and navigating the various challenges that may arise on the journey?

 # Conclusion

In this chapter, we explored how the PLC process can complement the IB PYP framework to enhance learning and teaching in transdisciplinary units of inquiry. The four PLC critical questions provide a valuable structure to ensure clarity on the learning goals throughout the unit. Additionally, these questions help guarantee learning engagements are responsive to student needs and interests while driving toward well-defined results. In some schools, IB PYP units of inquiry have a tendency to run adrift, and although units may be engaging, it can be difficult to determine the outcome of learning. With the PLC process guiding the discussions about the implementation of the unit, schools can better ensure rigor and adherence to a guaranteed and viable curriculum (Stuart et al., 2018). The next chapter will explore the PLC process within a single-subject unit of inquiry.

 # Next Steps

Consider the following suggested actions for getting started on becoming highly effective and then moving to the next level by becoming learning progressive.

Getting Started on Being Highly Effective

- Adopt or design a template on which to articulate the answers to PLC critical question one.

- Make sure to articulate answers to PLC critical questions one and two from the very beginning of each unit. Use these documentation tools in a responsive and proactive manner.

- Examine your timetable and restructure as needed to ensure collaborative teams have shared and adequate time to analyze and respond to data.

- Structure collaborative team meetings throughout the week so they allow for data inputting, individual and collective analysis, determination of how to respond to data, and then time to plan and gather resources.

- Implement the practice of having a planning retreat or long block of devoted time before starting each unit to fully unpack and project the unit.

Moving to the Next Level—Becoming Learning Progressive

- Enroll in a deep-dive course examining conceptual learning. Better yet, hire a consultant to work with your school in your context to help your staff gain collective understanding.

- Allow your students' interests, ideas, and passions to drive the unit of inquiry.

- Adopt a tool that encourages and supports mapping the personalized learning journey.

 # References and Resources

Biggs, J. (n.d.). *SOLO Taxonomy*. Accessed at https://johnbiggs.com.au/academic /solo-taxonomy on May 20, 2022.

Biggs, J. B., & Collis, K. F. (1982). *Evaluating the quality of learning: The SOLO Taxonomy*. New York: Academies Press.

DuFour, R., DuFour, R., Eaker, R., Many, T. W., & Mattos, M. (2016). *Learning by doing: A handbook for Professional Learning Communities at Work* (3rd ed.). Bloomington, IN: Solution Tree Press.

International Baccalaureate Organization. (2018a). *Collaborative planning process for learning and teaching*. Accessed at https://xmltwo.ibo.org/publications /PYP/p_0_pypxx_pip_1810_1/pdf/collaborative-planning-process-en.pdf on May 20, 2022.

International Baccalaureate Organization. (2018b). *Learning and teaching*. Accessed at https://resources.ibo.org/data/learning-and-teaching_899fc563-3f16 -4ad6-89c7-f60983c9d6d3/learning-and-teaching-en_bffd8f20-78b3-4d6e -83dc-7255d1bf1c29.pdf on May 20, 2022.

International Baccalaureate Organization. (2018c). *The learner.* Accessed at https://resources.ibo.org/data/the-learner_fc17a71a-2344-4b26-84cb -caca3a02750d/the-learner-en_d32875a1-8611-4de3-9f7d-14a22127adc2 .pdf on May 20, 2022.

International Baccalaureate Organization. (2022). *Our mission.* Accessed at https://www.ibo.org/about-the-ib/mission on May 20, 2022.

Stonefield Schools. (2022). *Our vision.* Accessed at https://stonefields.school.nz/our -school-vision on May 20, 2022.

Stuart, T. S., Heckmann, S., Mattos, M., & Buffum, A. (2018). *Personalized learning in a PLC at Work: Student agency through the four critical questions.* Bloomington, IN: Solution Tree Press.

Yodit Hizekiel is deputy elementary school principal at the International Community School (ICS) of Addis Ababa in Ethiopia. She is a former learning coach and team leader and has worked as a classroom teacher across the elementary grades during her career. Yodit has worked in public and private schools in the United States and internationally, focusing on the core subjects in elementary education and leadership, and on curricular work and staff professional development.

Yodit is a long-time member of Toastmasters International, having held leadership positions in her club as president, vice president of public relations, and sergeant at arms. She has won multiple speech contests, including international competitions. Yodit is also a workshop leader and has presented at the PLC at Work Institute in Addis Ababa, Ethiopia. She has been a runner-up Teacher of the Year and recipient of multiple Teacher of the Month awards. Yodit has a certificate of school management and leadership from the Harvard Graduate School of Education. In addition, she has completed training in a variety of areas of the PYP: student-centered coaching, reading and writing instruction, and mathematics.

Yodit received a bachelor's degree from Southwestern Assemblies of God University in Waxahachie, Texas, and a master's degree from the State University of New York, Buffalo. She is pursuing a doctorate in educational leadership at Wilkes University in Pennsylvania.

To book Yodit Hizekiel for professional development, contact pd@Solution Tree.com.

CHAPTER 3

Mathematics and Literacy in the PYP

Yodit Hizekiel

Transdisciplinary learning is one of the most important ideals in the International Baccalaureate Primary Years Programme (IB PYP) framework. The IB PYP states that *transdisciplinary learning* is "a fundamental PYP belief that for early and primary years learners, continuous integration and connection of prior and new knowledge and experiences is the most meaningful way to broaden their understanding about the world" (IBO, 2018a). When instruction is transdisciplinary, subjects connect seamlessly; it becomes unclear where one subject ends and another begins. As much as possible, literacy and mathematics concepts naturally flow and connect within a unit of inquiry as teachers and students focus on specific learning targets and goals. Student learning is paramount. In chapter 2 (page 21), you saw the big picture of how the IB PYP framework and the PLC process can work together as you aim for all students to learn at high levels. In this chapter, I examine how the PLC process informs literacy and mathematics instruction in an IB PYP school.

PLC Critical Question One and the PYP

Critical question one of the PLC process asks, "What do we want students to know, understand, and be able to do?" (DuFour, DuFour, Eaker, Many, & Mattos, 2016). In *Learning by Doing: A Handbook for Professional Learning Communities at Work*, PLC architects Richard DuFour and Robert Eaker and experts Rebecca DuFour, Thomas W. Many, and Mike Mattos (2016) state, "The question 'Learn what?' is one of the most significant questions the members of a PLC will consider"

(p. 113). They continue, "In fact, the entire PLC process is predicated on a deep understanding on the part of all educators of what all students must know and be able to do as a result of every unit of instruction" (DuFour et al., 2016, p. 113). In mathematics and literacy instruction, collaborative teams must spend time answering and clarifying the critical questions within the context of the IB PYP.

Answering the critical questions is one of the processes that ensures a guaranteed and viable curriculum; *guaranteed and viable* means students have access to the same essential learning outcomes regardless of who is teaching the class, and the curriculum can be taught in the time allotted (Marzano, Norford, Finn, & Finn, 2017).

When answering the first PLC critical question, teams clarify the exact expectations for student learning. In schools that use the Common Core State Standards or national, state, or provincial standards, it is a simple task of homing in on those skills, knowledge, and dispositions the standards already outline and then clarifying which ones students will address at a given time. Most schools in the United States use the Common Core State Standards to clarify grade-level expectations, as do many international schools.

When considering the Common Core standards, ensuring a guaranteed and viable curriculum becomes less straightforward. As research from Robert J. Marzano, Jennifer S. Norford, Michelle Finn, and Douglas Finn IIII (2017) shows, it is virtually impossible to address all the Common Core standards because there is just not enough time in a student's K–12 school career to address them all. This means there must be prioritization of standards (Eaker & Marzano, 2020).

The IB PYP framework allows schools to use whatever standards they like, but there are also scope-and-sequence documents for specific subject areas including language (English language arts in the Common Core) and mathematics (IBO, 2018a, 2018c). These scope-and-sequence documents are conceptually based and arranged in four or five phases, which are not grade-level correlations but rather, a progression of the depth of conceptual understandings. According to the PYP, *conceptual understandings* "have relevance across, between, and beyond the subject and [connect] a wide-ranging knowledge" (IBO, n.d.). Conceptual understandings are critical for student success and knowledge in a continuously expanding and changing world. It behooves educators to understand that the teaching and learning happening now must be applicable in the long term and the present. That is where concepts prove critical. Since content knowledge and skills required in many contexts are so quickly changing, what will have longevity are the concepts on which content knowledge and skills are organized, which can be transferred to new contexts of knowledge and skills. Consequently, the only way the learning teachers facilitate with students will prove applicable is when it is conceptual and allows for transference across emerging knowledge and skills.

The IB PYP is a concept-driven curriculum framework. The framework centers on seven key concepts and related concepts—the big, overarching understandings that are the goals for learning. The IB PYP states, "Concepts are powerful, broad and abstract organizing ideas that may be transdisciplinary or subject based. They represent the vehicle for student inquiry into the opportunities and challenges of local and global significance" (IBO, 2018e). In mathematics and literacy, concepts allow students to make connections, make meaning of what they are learning, and use those big, overarching understandings to make sense of the world through the lens of discrete subjects.

Most standards, however, are not conceptually based like in the IB PYP, but focus more on skills and knowledge. In applying the PLC process in an IB PYP framework, it becomes necessary to connect the skills and knowledge from the standards (such as the Common Core) to the conceptual understandings so the standards are all in service of the conceptual learning students should achieve. By answering PLC critical question one, teams decide on a set of the most critical standards to address. In the IB PYP, the next step is to connect those standards to the conceptual understanding they will serve (see figure 3.1).

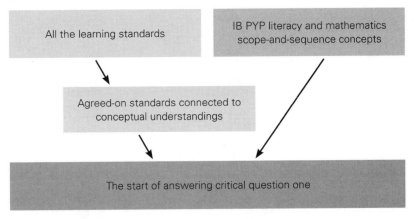

FIGURE 3.1: Connecting standards to IB PYP scope-and-sequence concepts.

One way of making this connection is by taking the focus standards and using the applicable IB PYP scope-and-sequence concepts to connect the two and clarify the answer to PLC critical question one.

Teachers who will be teaching the guaranteed and viable curriculum must go through the process of clarifying which standards are in service of which concepts. The second big idea that drives the PLC process is a collaborative culture and collective responsibility (DuFour et al., 2016), so this task is done collaboratively. As the collaborative team is also collectively responsible for *all* students learning, it is imperative for clarity about what specific learning the team is responsible for. During this practice, the specific concepts from the phases in the PYP scope-and-sequence documents will not align to a certain phase but will spread across two or maybe three phases, depending on the specific context of the school and students.

Language

For example, look at the Common Core English language arts (ELA) standards for a grade 3 classroom. Standards RL.3.1 and RL.3.3—the skills to learn—state respectively, "Ask and answer questions to demonstrate understanding of a text, referring explicitly to the text as a basis for the answers," and "Describe characters in a story (e.g., their traits, motivations, or feelings) and explain how their actions contribute to the sequence of events" (National Governors Association [NGA] Center for Best Practices & Council of Chief State School Officers [CCSSO], 2010a).

When looking at the language scope and sequence of the IB PYP, you'll see conceptual understandings that frame these skills: in phase three, the conceptual understanding, "Wondering about texts and asking questions helps us understand the meaning" and in phase four, "Reading and thinking work together to enable us to make meaning" (IBO, 2018a). Figure 3.2 shows what answers to PLC critical question one in the ELA classroom might look like.

PLC Critical Question One: What do we want all students to know, understand, and be able to do?		
Understand (Conceptual Understandings)		
Wondering about texts and asking questions helps us understand the meaning.		
Reading and thinking work together to enable us to make meaning.		
Characters' traits and decisions can drive the plot of a story.		
Know (Knowledge)	**Do (Skills)**	**Be (Dispositions)**
Understand how to describe the characters in a story. Characters' actions contribute to the sequence of events.	Wonder and ask questions about texts.	Inquirers Thinkers

FIGURE 3.2: Answers to PLC critical question one include conceptual understandings, knowledge, skills, and dispositions in a language unit.

Mathematics

Like ELA, answering critical question one in mathematics requires the same process of narrowing down the most essential standards, connecting them to the associated conceptual understandings, and clarifying the learning goal. For example, take a grade 3 unit on fractions. You may determine that one of the most essential standards is 3.NF.1, "Understand a fraction $1/b$ as a quantity formed by 1 part when a whole is partitioned into b equal parts; understand a fraction a/b as the quantity formed by parts of size $1/b$" and perhaps 3.NF.3, "Explain equivalence of fractions in special cases, and compare fractions by reasoning about their size" (NGA & CCSSO, 2010b). When considering the larger conceptual understanding of what knowledge and skills are transferable on the scope-and-sequence documents, you find the conceptual understanding, "Fractions, decimal fractions, and percentages are ways of representing whole-part relationships" (IBO, 2018c). Therefore, the concepts that will drive this unit will be the understanding that fraction language is used to understand the relationship between whole and part. Unpacking the answer to critical question one for these standards might look like the example in figure 3.3.

PLC Critical Question One: What do we want all students to know, understand, and be able to do?		
Understand (Conceptual Understandings)		
Fractions, decimal fractions, and percentages are ways of representing whole-part relationships.		
Know (Knowledge)	**Do (Skills)**	**Be (Dispositions)**
Understand what a fraction is and what it represents. Fractions can be represented using different numbers. The size of fractions can be used to compare them.	Model and explain what fractions are. Relate fractions to the whole. Model and write equivalent fractions. Use fraction sizes to reason and compare fractions.	Thinkers Communicators

FIGURE 3.3: Answers to PLC critical question one include conceptual understandings, knowledge, skills, and dispositions in a mathematics unit.

In considering the use of both conceptual understandings and specific skill and knowledge standards, it is important to note the IB PYP scope-and-sequence documents "provide information for the whole school community of learning that is going on in the subject of mathematics" (IBO, 2018c), and likewise in language arts. So, there are other conceptual understandings not explicitly stated in the IB PYP documents that a school could decide are important and worthy of inclusion in the curriculum. Both the IB PYP framework and the PLC process assume educators contextualize those processes to provide the best and highest quality of learning for students.

Student Agency

While teachers are answering the four critical questions, students can also answer the same questions on their own. As students answer, "What do I want to know, understand, and be able to do?" (Stuart, Heckmann, Mattos, & Buffum, 2018), they define what the learning goal is for them. In the same way that teachers prioritize the standards, connect the conceptual understandings that lead to transfer, and then divide those into the individual learning targets, students do the same as they answer PLC critical question one.

This might look like students reflecting on a preassessment and deciding what it is that they need to work on or creating a personal schedule as they plan how they will spend their day (see figure 3.4). To make this happen, students must know the applicable mathematics and literacy progressions, which should be written in student-friendly language that is easy for students to understand.

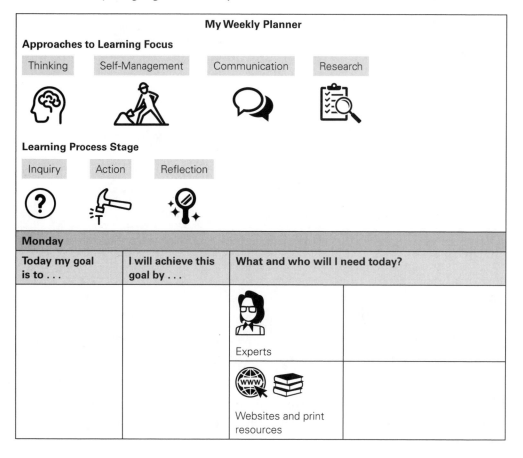

		Tools and materials	
		A place	
		Other	

Source: © 2021 by International Community School of Addis Ababa. Adapted with permission.

FIGURE 3.4: Student weekly planner.

*Visit **go.SolutionTree.com/PLCbooks** for a free reproducible version of this figure.*

PLC Critical Question Two and the PYP

PLC critical question two asks, "How will we know if they learned it?" (DuFour et al., 2016). This question refers to the ongoing formative and data-gathering assessments that provide evidence of learning. To do this, collaborative teams in PLCs develop and use common formative assessments that align to the skills, knowledge, and dispositions they identified when answering PLC critical question one. The implementation of these common assessments will determine the next steps in each student's learning, so it is critical teachers assess learning formatively so they can adjust as the class progresses through the unit. This is particularly important when considering that mathematics and literacy skills build on each other and deepen in the rigor and depth, making mastery and understanding critical. The same applies to the conceptual understanding in the IB PYP.

The purpose of assessment in both the PLC process and IB PYP framework is to inform teaching and learning in a continuous and cyclical process in which teams gather and analyze data. The IB PYP outlines assessment as having four dimensions: (1) monitoring learning, (2) documenting learning, (3) measuring learning, and (4) reporting learning (IBO, n.d.). For the purposes of this book, implementation of the PLC process in mathematics and literacy in the IB PYP, educators only focus on monitoring and documenting learning (data gathering) involved in this process.

Once the team defines and clarifies the essential knowledge, skills, and dispositions for the unit, educators must build and create assessments that measure and provide evidence of learning of those learning targets. The third big idea of the PLC process is a *results orientation* (DuFour et al., 2016); this means that ways to evaluate and measure learning must follow all the clarification and specific goal setting. To this end, teams must define and outline specific processes to obtain evidence of student learning. If teams focus on results, they must clarify what success looks like, what learning can look like, and how it might look when there is proof of learning. That's why collaborative teams in PLCs need to ask and answer critical question three.

In the IB PYP and in educational best practice, students are involved in the assessment process, reflecting on their learning, receiving and acting on feedback, and setting goals for their learning; and teachers reflect on practice, offer timely and specific feedback, and adjust practices to support better learning (IBO, 2018d). This practice is done in collaboration with the PLC process.

For some people, the word *assessments* conjures up images of worksheets and essays. However, assessments are not always pencil-and-paper tasks students engage in. Especially when considering the assessment of concepts, pencil-and-paper tasks may not be the best way for students to demonstrate their learning. For example, the teacher asks students to demonstrate the concept, *People write to communicate.* The teacher could ask a series of questions to see if students can share that concept, but it would be far better to provide learning experiences and engagements where students demonstrate the benefits and necessity to communicate in writing, thereby providing an authentic context to evidence their understanding.

But the big question remains: How do educators assess conceptual understandings? In her book *Tools for Teaching Conceptual Understanding*, author Julie Stern (2018) emphasizes that the goal is learning that transfers to new and novel situations, and progress is more important than mastery as a student's understanding of the concept continues to deepen. It seems, then, that traditional assessment methods may fall short of reaching that goal; rather, student reflection and self-assessment, along with goal setting (and teacher support as needed), may be more on target.

One tool teams and educators can use to assist in assessing conceptual understandings is the SOLO (structure of observed learning outcomes) Taxonomy (Biggs & Collis, 1982). This classification allows for identifying increasingly complex levels of understanding. The levels are as follows.

- **Prestructural:** The student does not know about the concept and has no ideas about the concept.

- **Unistructural:** The student can articulate or demonstrate one thing about the concept but no more than that; understanding is very basic.

- **Multistructural:** The student can articulate or demonstrate a few ideas about the concept and has an organizing structure or understanding of how the ideas relate or connect to one another.

- **Relational:** The student can connect ideas as they increase in complexity, understand their relationships to one another, and see the bigger conceptual picture and overall meaning.

- **Extended abstract:** The student can take the understanding and complexities of the concept and connect this learning to new situations; the student can generalize, infer, and apply the understanding, which is transfer—the ultimate goal.

Language

Particularly in literacy, teams can address PLC critical question two in a way that honors the learning and allows for documenting learning. Take the example of the learning target from grade 3 shared in the section on critical question one (page 39). Educators can monitor and document student learning using a simple multiple-choice or short-answer assignment; however, this does not support the PYP philosophy that assessments must be authentic, interactive, and collaborative (IBO, 2018a). For learners, the assessment is not a simple test of their learning; it might be a group of students reading a book together and having a genuine conversation about what is happening in the book. A student asks a question about a character. Another student answers the question and adds his thoughts, while another student asks for clarification. The student clarifies, and another student gives more support. Another student shares her thinking, and the learning continues. Meanwhile, the teacher is listening to this conversation, and when necessary, jumps in briefly to push students' thinking or add prompting and questioning to deepen the conversation. This conversation *is* data. The teacher observes student understanding in the conversation and documents the data in preparation for analysis and next steps, according to the PLC process.

Before students have their conversation about the book, the collaborative team must clarify what the teachers will be listening for in the conversation that will show understanding of the learning targets. This might include a conferring form with look-fors and learning objectives and a form for documenting the learning and understandings each student shows. Using the SOLO Taxonomy in literacy shows the ways a student can progress in those learning goals (Biggs & Collis, 1982).

A literacy example based on one of the conceptual understandings from the previous section appears in figure 3.5.

PLC Critical Question Two: How will we know if they learned it?					
Understandings to be assessed	(I need help to generate an idea.)	Unistructural (I have one idea.)	(I have many ideas.)	Relational (I can connect my ideas.)	Extended Abstract (I can take my ideas further.)
Conceptual understandings: Wondering about texts and asking questions help us understand the meaning. Characters' traits and decisions can drive the plot of a story.	No ideas	Asking and answering simple plot questions	Using questions to ask further questions	Relating character actions to following events and traits of other characters and the plot	Using those same skills when watching a television show or in daily life

FIGURE 3.5: Sample SOLO Taxonomy for literature.

As the teacher is conferring or listening to student conversations about the text, the teacher will be able to identify the depth of understanding students demonstrate through their interactions with other students. The teacher will then take these data to the collaborative team.

Mathematics

When it comes to mathematics, the process is similar. Learning and understanding mathematics conceptually are paramount for students because they involve deep understanding that leads to success, especially when there is gradual depth of complexity as students get older. However, the skills needed in mathematics build on prior knowledge and skills. Ensuring students sufficiently understand those prerequisite mathematics skills is critical for future mathematics achievement.

Similarly, when creating common mathematics assessments in the PLC process, educators need to be mindful of important ideas related to mathematics learning and assessment. For example, clarifying the appropriate levels of conceptual understanding means students are learning at the developmentally appropriate levels of skill and conceptual understanding, and consistently using modeling and manipulatives, and then asking students to share their thinking; this provides insight into the level and complexity of their understanding. This is best done through problem-solving practices that allow educators to observe multiple facets of mathematics understanding. A mathematics example based on one of the conceptual understandings appears in figure 3.6.

PLC Critical Question Two: How will we know if they've learned it?					
Understandings to be assessed	(I need help to generate an idea.)	Unistructural (I have one idea.)	(I have many ideas.)	Relational (I can connect my ideas.)	Extended Abstract (I can take my ideas further.)
Conceptual Understandings: Fractions represent the equal parts of a whole. The numbers in a fraction communicate different elements of the parts of a whole.	No ideas	Recognizing fractions	Determining if something is a true fraction and matching a written representation to a picture representation	Explaining what a fraction is with its key characteristics	Applying IB PYP understanding of equal parts to new situations and problems

FIGURE 3.6: Sample SOLO Taxonomy for mathematics.

Student Agency

As educators personalize the PLC process for students and honor the agency of learners in mathematics and literacy in the IB PYP framework, they need to interpret the learning goals and targets into learning progressions that allow students to be in control of their learning, accelerating and decelerating their rate of learning based on their aptitudes and learning needs (Stuart et al., 2018). "It is vital that the learning targets and curriculum are accessible to students to support agency and ownership" (Stuart et al., 2018, p. 76). It is also important for teachers to make conceptual understandings accessible to students because this learning will transfer across contexts. When addressing PLC critical question two, students can see and track their learning across literacy and mathematics, making them better equipped to self-assess accurately and set learning goals independently because they can see the trajectory for their learning and take ownership of their own progress.

Schools around the world, and in particular international schools, are making an environment conducive to this level of personalization by creating learning spaces and structures that support student voice, choice, and ownership. *Learning hubs* are such spaces. Structures include students being able to choose the scheduling of their day and what they will be learning based on the learning progressions, which they also have access to. PLC critical question two has students asking, "How will I know if I have learned it?" (Stuart et al., 2018). Then, according to the processes in the learning hub, students organize their day around which learning targets they will be working on and how they intend to show they are learning.

PLC Critical Questions Three and Four and the PYP

Critical question three of the PLC process asks, "What will we do when they are not learning?" (DuFour et al., 2016). In answering question two, teams have already set acceptable criteria for evidence of learning. When teams get to the third question, they should be asking, "Now what?" Teachers should not file away data that show students are not learning and then report later. Learning is a cyclical process where data direct next moves. The Now what? question allows teams to make decisions and moves to intervene with students who are not learning.

Similarly, critical question four asks, "What will we do if they already know it?" (DuFour et al., 2016). Teams have already set the criteria for what success looks like when answering critical question two. When teams have evidence showing students have learned it, those data tell teams they need another plan for those students— plans for how they might extend their learning. Teams also address this fourth question in a cyclical fashion. Educators put students at a disadvantage if they are not specifically planning extensions for students who show proficiency. How are educators making sure all students are learning at high levels if they are not allowing for high-level learning at whatever depth and breadth students require?

Although transdisciplinary learning characterizes teaching in an IB PYP, the framework recognizes there are times when it is necessary to group students about a specific learning target to best meet the needs of those students. This includes students who require an extension in their learning. This clearly includes when the data show students need subject-specific intervention or extension in literacy and mathematics concepts. Grouping for targeted instruction may be a good way to meet the needs of students requiring intervention, but instruction that involves student agency and personalized pathways to extension and intervention is also a viable way of meeting those students' needs.

Creating or finding the time required for addressing PLC critical questions three and four can prove difficult in some situations and schools because of scheduling and availability of teachers. This challenge is not unique in international schools; it is one schools all over the world face. However, these questions, like questions one and two, are non-negotiable. Collaborative teams cycle through the questions on a regular basis, constantly asking, making adjustments, looking at the data, and adjusting, and asking again. Planning out appropriate interventions, reteaching opportunities, and extensions is a defining outcome of the cycle.

One way to ensure teams have time to answer critical questions three and four is to create schoolwide schedules that allow for specific time to address student needs the data show. Many schools around the world create time and space in their schedule during the school day for students to receive targeted interventions in the areas in which they demonstrate need, while other students engage in extensions to learning that can be personalized, allowing for maximum student agency. This time, specifically set apart during the day, guarantees the necessary interventions will take place and students who don't show a learning need can engage in additional learning that extends their understanding. Response to intervention experts Austin Buffum, Mike Mattos, and Janet Malone (2018) call this *flex time*, but this idea has many other names as well. At the International Community School (ICS) of Addis Ababa, we call it *grow time*, so students and educators understand that growth is expected to happen at that time, wherever a student might be on their learning journey. Chapter 4 (page 59) discusses the idea of grow time and intervention in more detail.

Learning is personalized when students are in charge and in control of their own learning, and when they are asking and answering the four critical questions for themselves to progress along a pathway of learning (Stuart et al., 2018). Personalization should not be something reserved only for those who have already learned it; rather, all students should have the opportunity to personalize their learning. Ultimately, all students need to learn at high levels, and when students have voice, choice, and ownership of their learning, educators can produce future-ready, lifelong learners (Stuart et al., 2018).

By asking "What should I do when I'm not learning?" and "What should I do when I have already learned it?" students can set their own goals and targets to demonstrate agency in their learning. When addressing critical question four, students can engage in authentic choice of tasks, curiosity projects, and alternative ways of exploring their interests and curiosities. For example, students may decide after learning about characters in books that they want to create a character themselves. Perhaps they decide the character needs to come alive in a multimedia project, so they will need to learn how to do that. Perhaps at that point, they realize this character can be a schoolwide mascot or spokesperson. The students must then consider what the character will say. There is no end to the possibilities that lie ahead when students are in control.

While focusing on the concepts, skills, and knowledge of reading and mathematics, students also need to focus on the dispositions. In the IB PYP, the approaches to learning (ATLs) summarize these dispositions. As coauthors Robert Eaker and Robert J. Marzano (2020) state in *Professional Learning Communities at Work and High Reliability Schools*, "In addition to foundational skills, students must—first and foremost—develop higher thinking skills" (p. 282). So as students ask critical questions three and four in the areas of mathematics and literacy while their teachers are also asking them, progression along the ATLs is the backdrop of the subject-specific learning. As a result, a progression of those learning-to-learn skills is needed so students can keep track of their learning, not just in mathematics and literacy skills, but in the ATLs. Figure 3.7 shows an example of one such progression.

Research Skills: Where are you?					
Ask questions.	I can notice things around me and ask questions about what I observe.	I can use my observations to create a specific question.	I can use my observations to create a specific question that relates to a problem or issue.	I can create a research question about a problem or issue.	I can create a research question to investigate a problem or issue.

Select relevant sources.	I can pick out a few important details from a source.	I can choose one source that relates to the topic or question. I can identify some details from the source that relate to my topic or question.	I can choose one or more sources that relate to the topic or question. I can identify more important details from the source that relate to my topic or question.	I can find multiple sources that relate to my topic or research question.	I can use keyword searches to find multiple sources that relate to my topic or research question. I can gather important information from multiple sources that provides evidence or details related to my topic or research question.
Organize information from multiple sources.	I can express something new I learned.	I can make a connection between what I knew and what I now know based on a source.	I can make more than one new connection between the topic or question and the key information I identify from one or more sources.	I can compare information from multiple sources that directly informs my topic or research question.	I can compare information from multiple sources that answers my topic or research question. I can use details from the sources to explain insights I have formed about my topic or research question.

FIGURE 3.7: Sample showing a possible progression for research skills.

Finally, as they take ownership of their own learning and engage in the cycle of learning, students with agency must keep track of their learning. One way they can do this is by using a goal-setting form (see figure 3.8, page 54). Students reflect on their progress and make a plan for what's next, considering the ATLs as the main measurement of their progress and taking their learning all the way to the action (that is, applying it in their lives or taking steps to serve others based on their own learning and initiative), another important aspect of the PYP (IBO, 2018d).

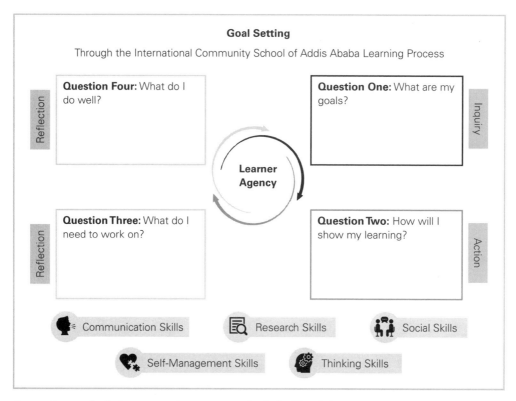

Goal Setting

Through the International Community School of Addis Ababa Learning Process

Source: © 2021 by the International Community School of Addis Ababa. Adapted with permission.

FIGURE 3.8: Goal setting through the ICS learning process.

Visit **go.SolutionTree.com/PLCbooks** for a free reproducible version of this figure.

Conclusion

The pairing of the IB PYP framework and the PLC process enables schools to reach the goal of all students learning at high levels (not just facts and skills); their learning also equips students for a world yet imagined. In an IB PYP school, students learn mathematics and literacy in a real-world context and in practical terms, rather than in isolation and unconnected to real life. The PLC process ensures that when students don't learn and when they do learn, teachers and students take further actions based on data to continue learning. Educators working collaboratively with results in mind guide this process. Learning is the goal, and with collective responsibility, a focus on student success, and a clear focus on those skills, students will learn how to learn.

Next Steps

Consider the following suggested actions for getting started on becoming highly effective and then moving to the next level by becoming learning progressive.

Getting Started on Being Highly Effective

- Collaboratively clarify the agreed-on standards in mathematics and literacy that are non-negotiable for each grade level.

- Connect standards to the conceptual understanding they are in service of, possibly from the IB PYP scope-and-sequence documents. What are the transferable big understandings you are aiming for?

- Decide on and commit to a common assessment tool or process for assessing conceptual understanding that teams will use to create common formative assessments to guide next steps and instruction as you go through the PLC process.

- Begin to create learning continuums that allow for personalized learning.

- Engage in considerable unpacking of your previous processes to ensure a common understanding within and across teams.

Moving to the Next Level—Becoming Learning Progressive

- Define and clarify learning continuums in mathematics and literacy along which students can progress as they achieve agency.

- Clarify and communicate the agreed-on mathematics and literacy standards to and with students so they also have a clear understanding of the skills, concepts, and dispositions, and of the learning continuums that clarify the learning.

- Establish systems that allow students to take ownership of their learning in mathematics and literacy (such as weekly planners and student-owned schedules), as they progress along those learning continuums and ask and answer the four PLC critical questions themselves.

References and Resources

Biggs, J. B., & Collis, K. F. (1982). *Evaluating the quality of learning: The SOLO Taxonomy*. New York: Academies Press.

Buffum, A., Mattos, M., & Malone, J. (2018). *Taking action: A handbook for RTI at Work*. Bloomington, IN: Solution Tree Press.

DuFour, R., DuFour, R., Eaker, R., Many, T. W., & Mattos, M. (2016). *Learning by doing: A handbook for Professional Learning Communities at Work* (3rd ed.). Bloomington, IN: Solution Tree Press.

DuFour, R., DuFour, R., Eaker, R., Mattos, M., & Muhammad, A. (2021). *Revisiting Professional Learning Communities at Work: Proven insights for sustained, substantive school improvement* (2nd ed.). Bloomington, IN: Solution Tree Press.

Eaker, R., & Marzano, R. J. (Eds.). (2020). *Professional Learning Communities at Work and High Reliability Schools: Cultures of continuous learning*. Bloomington, IN: Solution Tree Press.

International Baccalaureate Organization. (n.d.). *Primary Years Programme*. Accessed at www.ibo.org/programmes/primary-years-programme on April 15, 2022.

International Baccalaureate Organization. (2018a). *Language scope and sequence*. Accessed at www.ibo.org on May 20, 2022.

International Baccalaureate Organization. (2018b). *Learning and teaching*. Accessed at https://resources.ibo.org/data/learning-and-teaching_899fc563-3f16 -4ad6-89c7-f60983c9d6d3/learning-and-teaching-en_bffd8f20-78b3-4d6e -83dc-7255d1bf1c29.pdf on May 20, 2022.

International Baccalaureate Organization. (2018c). *Mathematics scope and sequence*. Accessed at www.ibo.org on May 20, 2022.

International Baccalaureate Organization. (2018d). *The learner*. Accessed at https://resources.ibo.org/data/the-learner_fc17a71a-2344-4b26-84cb -caca3a02750d/the-learner-en_d32875a1-8611-4de3-9f7d-14a22127adc2 .pdf on May 20, 2022.

International Baccalaureate Organization. (2018e). *The learning community*. Accessed at https://ibo.org/programmes/primary-years-programme/curriculum /the-learning-community on May 20, 2022.

Marzano, R. J. (2017). *The new art and science of teaching.* Bloomington, IN: Solution Tree Press.

Marzano, R. J., Norford, J. S., Finn, M., & Finn, D, III. (2017). *A handbook for personalized competency-based education.* Bloomington, IN: Marzano Resources.

National Governors Association Center for Best Practices & Council of Chief State School Officers. (2010a). *Common Core State Standards for English language arts and literacy in history/social studies, science, and technical subjects.* Washington, DC: Authors. Accessed at www.corestandards.org/assets/CCSSI_ELA%20Standards.pdf on June 29, 2022.

National Governors Association Center for Best Practices & Council of Chief State School Officers. (2010b). *Common Core State Standards for mathematics.* Washington, DC: Authors. Accessed at www.corestandards.org/assets/CCSSI_Math%20Standards.pdf on June 29, 2022.

Stern, J. (2018). *Tools for teaching conceptual understanding (Elementary): Harvesting natural curiosity for learning that transfers.* Thousand Oaks, CA: Corwin Press.

Stuart, T. S., Heckmann, S., Mattos, M., & Buffum, A. (2018). *Personalized learning in a PLC at Work: Student agency through the four critical questions.* Bloomington, IN: Solution Tree Press.

Jacqueline Olin is a learning support teacher at the International Community School (ICS) of Addis Ababa in Ethiopia. Her role is to support the diverse learning needs of students in the context of a professional learning community (PLC) utilizing a response to intervention (RTI) approach. She has been teaching since 2007, teaching grades 4 and 5, with prior experience teaching in grades 1 and 3. Her other international teaching experience includes teaching grade 4 at the QSI International School of Minsk in Belarus and at QSI Almaty International School in Kazakhstan. Before teaching internationally, she worked as a learning resource center teacher at an elementary school in Oregon.

Jacqueline is an active participant in collaborative team meetings and school trainings at ICS Addis Ababa. At PLC at Work institutes, she has co-led workshops regarding how working as a PLC helps to personalize learning and meet the diverse needs of learners.

Jacqueline received a bachelor's degree in education with dual endorsements in special education and elementary education from Western Washington University and a master's degree in multidisciplinary studies from State University of New York Buffalo State College.

To book Jacqueline Olin for professional development, contact pd@Solution Tree.com.

CHAPTER 4

Response to Intervention in the PYP

Jacqueline Olin

The third critical question of a PLC, "What do we do when students have not learned it?" allows collaborative teams to address a variety of educational needs for students (DuFour, DuFour, Eaker, Many, & Mattos, 2016). Any effective school supports student needs through a multitiered system of supports, such as response to intervention (RTI). Statistics show how more traditional methods of addressing learning gaps have proven ineffective. In 2019, the graduation rate in the United States for students receiving special education was 14 percent lower than the national rate (National Center for Education Statistics [NCES], 2019). Too often, special education students do not go to college and are disproportionately represented in prisons (DuFour, DuFour, Eaker, Mattos, & Muhammad, 2021). RTI offers a viable alternative to this *wait to fail* service-delivery model. Coauthors George M. Batsche, José M. Castillo, Decia N. Dixon, and Susan Forde (2008) illuminate the reality educators face:

> In the average school system, there are 330 minutes in the instructional day, 1,650 minutes in the instructional week, and 56,700 minutes in the instructional year. Except in unusual circumstances, these are the only minutes we have to provide effective services for students. The number of years we have to apply these minutes is fixed. Therefore, each minute counts, and schools cannot afford to support inefficient models of service delivery. (p. 177)

Educators must prioritize what works in schools and move forward with knowledge and courage. Studies and research provide schools with both direction and a responsibility to ensure all students learn at high levels. According to the work of researcher John Hattie (2012), collective teacher efficacy, along with RTI, rank at the top of factors related to student achievement. This means an effective professional learning community (PLC) that embraces an RTI model will have some of the highest yields in student learning. RTI is so powerful, in fact, Hattie's (2012) research deems it *twice* as effective as any environmental factor that impacts student success. Consequently, educators should be spending *more* time on providing systematic and timely interventions for students during the school day than they spend discussing a student's home environment. Priorities matter if every student is to learn and succeed.

While considering priorities, educators also must consider equity in education. Students' educational fate should not simply depend on the teacher to whom they are assigned. RTI offers an equitable solution. It not only provides students with a system of support but also teachers with a network of support. One teacher does not have all the expertise or time to make the difference necessary for each student in the teacher's classroom. When educators implement RTI properly, especially in a PLC, there are many qualified individuals working together to ensure students each receive the support they need.

Ultimately, educators can view RTI as part of the greater purpose and calling of educators. RTI at Work experts Austin Buffum, Mike Mattos, and Chris Weber (2010) provide the following insight:

> The secret to capturing the right way of thinking about RTI comes down to answering this question: Why are we implementing Response to Intervention? The answer lies in why we joined this profession in the first place—to help children. Our work must be driven by the knowledge that our collaborative efforts will help determine the success or failure of our students. RTI should not be a program to raise student test scores, but rather a process to realize students' hopes and dreams. It should not be a way to meet state mandates, but a means to serve humanity. Once we understand the urgency of our work and embrace this noble cause as our fundamental purpose, how could we possibly allow any student to fail? (p. 16)

This chapter discusses the role of RTI and the PLC process to support students with special needs in an IB PYP school, from restructuring daily schedules and adjusting staffing to support approaches and the role of the teaching team.

This chapter explores questions to ask and actions to take to ensure students are learning at high levels. Examples and explanations show how RTI is a complementary and vital component to any organization committed to preparing students with the skills they need to succeed in an ever-changing world. Educators will learn processes and tools they can use or adapt to their school context. These processes and tools have been successful in international school settings specifically, but educators can use them in any school looking to increase the collective efficacy of teachers and student learning.

RTI

RTI is also called *response to instruction* and *responsiveness to intervention*. It is a multitiered instructional delivery model conceptually like tiered medical models of service delivery. For the purposes of this book, RTI is best understood as a process that offers every student:

> The additional time and support needed to learn at high levels. RTI's underlying premise is that schools should not delay providing help for struggling students until they fall far enough behind to qualify for special education, but instead should provide timely, targeted, systematic interventions to all students who demonstrate the need. (Buffum, Mattos, & Weber, 2012, p. xiii)

As stated previously, RTI is best worked out in the context of a PLC as it naturally allows for the levels of collaboration and problem solving required to be responsive to students' needs. RTI helps organize and operationalize the four critical questions that frame the work of a PLC. Asking and answering these critical questions require an understanding of the different tiers of instruction, as well as the roles and responsibilities within those tiers. To facilitate this understanding, many often view RTI as an inverted pyramid (see figure 4.1, page 62).

The first tier of instruction is the *guaranteed and viable curriculum*, which all students have access to (guaranteed) and is doable in the time allotted (viable). These are the essential standards, understandings, and skills students each must learn for the next grade or step in their educational career. This is the answer to PLC critical question one, What do we want students to know, understand, and be able to do? (DuFour et al., 2016). It's important to note that students with learning gaps still need access to Tier 1 grade-level content so they are not continually falling behind.

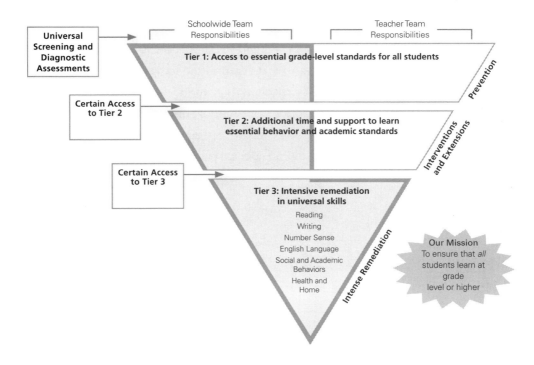

Source: Buffum, Mattos, & Malone, 2018.

FIGURE 4.1: The RTI at Work pyramid.

It is likely these students will need accommodations to access this content, especially if they have gaps in the universal skills for learning, which I discuss later in this chapter.

Most students will learn at an appropriate level and rate when teachers teach core instruction using research-based strategies. Some students (generally 10–15 percent), however, will need more time or more strategies to learn the key concepts and skills. These students will need a second layer of instruction beyond the core, also known as *Tier 2 instruction* or *intervention*. Classroom teachers are the experts at knowing which Tier 1 skills students did not master the first time. Therefore, these teachers must be highly engaged in making decisions regarding Tier 2 interventions. These interventions should be based on the essential Tier 1 skills or concepts the student is missing. Students will likely move in and out of Tier 2 intervention groups throughout the school year.

Not every student comes to school ready to master the grade-level (Tier 1) curriculum, and even the best Tier 2 interventions will not bring these students up to speed. Nearly every classroom has students who have not yet mastered the building blocks, or foundational skills, they need. There are a variety of reasons students may be missing these essential skills, but without them, it is impossible to expect students to learn at high levels. A school can efficiently use universal screeners, teacher observations, attendance records, and so on within the RTI model and PLC process to identify and support these students so gaps do not continue to widen. Coauthors Austin Buffum, Mike Mattos, and Janet Malone (2018) provide a summary of these foundational skills, which are sometimes called *universal skills of learning*:

1. Decode and comprehend grade-level text
2. Write effectively
3. Apply number sense
4. Comprehend the English language (or the school's primary language)
5. Consistently demonstrate social and academic behaviors
6. Overcome complications due to health or home (p. 22)

These foundational skills are Tier 3 in the RTI pyramid. In this third tier, specialists such as an English as an additional language (EAL) teacher, a learning support specialist, a special education teacher, a counselor, and an administrator may be involved in the coordination or delivery of services. Some students will only remain in this third tier for a short time (if the learning gap is simply due to lack of instruction and they respond quickly); however, other students may require this level of support for an extended period, perhaps even throughout their educational career. What's important to remember is these students also need core Tier 1 and Tier 2 instruction in addition to their Tier 3 support. Without core Tier 1 and Tier 2 instruction, they will continue to fall further behind.

Key Ideas for Effectively Implementing RTI

Applying and integrating these three tiers of instruction may sound complicated or even impossible, yet it is possible when a school is a highly functioning PLC. Coordinating and delivering services for students do not rest solely on one team or one person; these are collective responsibilities of all educators in the PLC. For RTI to be effective in a PLC, school leaders must reflect on their current practices to see if they align with essential elements of RTI. Figure 4.2 (page 64) is a tool to help a school self-assess whether their current practices support adopting an RTI model. Also, the RTI Action Network (www.rtinetwork.org) has many checklists and rubrics schools developed to guide their implementation of RTI.

Essential Element of RTI	Our Current Reality	Our Desired Outcome (Long-Term Goal)	Our First Steps (Short-Term Goal)
Have we embraced that RTI is not a special education or regular education program, but rather a schoolwide process that requires collective responsibility to ensure that all students learn?			
Is our instructional program standards-based and research-based?			
Is our instructional program delivered with fidelity by highly qualified teachers?			
Do we universally screen all students with comprehensive literacy and mathematics assessments several times a year?			
Do we frequently progress monitor students at risk in all tiers?			
Do we know when to provide students more intensive support?			
Do we communicate regularly with parents and other stakeholders?			

Source: Buffum, Mattos, & Weber, 2009, p. 172.

FIGURE 4.2: How do our school's current practices align with the essential elements of RTI?

*Visit **go.SolutionTree.com/PLCbooks** for a free reproducible version of this figure.*

Once a school is ready to implement RTI, there are two approaches most will take: a protocol approach or a problem-solving approach (Buffum, Mattos, & Weber, 2009). A *protocol approach* is a way of offering established interventions according to a set of criteria to address the learning gap (for example, a reading fluency intervention for students with poor reading fluency).

The training, progress monitoring, and decision making involved in a protocol approach are relatively straightforward. Some examples of intervention programs schools may use with a protocol approach include Read Naturally (https://
readnaturally.com), Leveled Literacy Intervention (https://fountasandpinnell
.com/lli), and Bridges Math Intervention (https://mathlearningcenter.org/curriculum
/bridges-intervention). The number of programs and trained staff in the school limits
the protocol approach. The *problem-solving approach*, on the other hand, allows for
more targeted plans with more staff input, making it far more individualized. This
model involves more collaboration and more complex training, progress monitoring, and decision making. The RTI approach a school will start with will likely be
based on the school's context, but I recommend schools eventually move toward a
blend of the protocol and problem-solving approaches. Schools can use figure 4.3
to decide which approach is best for their context, as well as how to respond to key
RTI questions.

Key Questions of RTI	Our Current Reality	Our Desired Outcome (Long-Term Goal)	Our First Steps (Short-Term Goal)
How many tiers of intervention can our school provide?			
How will our school identify students in need of support?			
Will our school employ the problem-solving approach, the protocol approach, or a blended approach?			
How will we define what determines an adequate response to intervention?			
What is the function of special education when implementing RTI?			

Source: Buffum et al., 2009, p. 173.

FIGURE 4.3: How will our school respond to key RTI questions?

*Visit **go.SolutionTree.com/PLCbooks** for a free reproducible version of this figure.*

Utilizing an RTI model in a PLC allows for both interventions (answering PLC critical question three, How will we respond when some students don't learn?) and extensions (answering PLC critical question four, How will we extend the learning for students who are already proficient?; DuFour et al., 2016), making the model become more fluid and manageable. It is both invaluable and possible to work with other experts to go student by student and skill by skill to ensure all students receive the support they need. All students need access to the core (Tier 1) curriculum. Any intervention or extension happens in addition to this instruction. Specifically, *intervention* includes what a school does for a student above and beyond what all students receive to help that student succeed academically (Buffum et al., 2018). An *extension* is what a school offers when educators need to challenge students beyond the grade-level curriculum or when students show they are ready to achieve higher levels of proficiency (Buffum et al., 2018). Sometimes the term *extension* is confused with the term *enrichment*; this book, however, makes a distinction between the two. *Enrichment* refers to the subjects that specials or elective teachers usually teach, such as art, music, physical education, and so on (Buffum et al., 2018). It is important that all students have access to enrichment and are not pulled from core instruction for intervention. Missing out on enrichment opportunities to receive interventions can create a lack of motivation and equity among students.

Anyone who has experience working in schools knows that implementing new models and frameworks is a process. As a school is developing as a PLC and adopting an RTI model, school leaders can begin to set benchmarks and aim for higher levels of implementation fidelity each year. Just as leaders expect students to grow and learn at high levels, they also expect schools and educators to grow. A school with a focus on learning at high levels will use research and take action to improve. According to Buffum and colleagues (2018), for an organization to successfully implement RTI, it must take these five essential actions:

1. Establish a guiding coalition.
2. Build a culture of collective responsibility.
3. Form collaborative teacher teams.
4. Create time for collaboration.
5. Commit to team norms. (p. 35)

A great first step for a school to successfully implement RTI is to ensure it builds a culture of collective responsibility. This is part of the second big idea of a PLC (DuFour et al., 2016). It is essential for a school to hire people who approach education with the belief that all students can learn at high levels. This does *not* mean educators must ensure every student has the same outcome or future. For example, in inclusive schools, students with severe or profound disabilities will likely not achieve in a similar manner as their typically developing peers. It's important to keep in mind that the percentage of the population with severe or profound disabilities is extremely small, and their program of support will look very different from the vast majority. For the purposes of this book, when the authors say *all* students can learn at high levels, they are referring to students who have the potential to live independently as an adult in the future (DuFour et al., 2016). Schools must hire people who believe that if a student is to live independently one day, that student can learn at high levels, and teachers must act on this belief.

So far in this chapter, I have discussed some key concepts and action steps related to RTI. Educators gain even more clarity about these ideas by understanding what RTI is *not*. It is *not* a new way to identify students for special education. It is *not* a formula or program you can buy. It is *not* a class or extra tutoring that educators add on to extend the length of an already busy school day. Instead, *RTI* is a model of service delivery that happens during regular school hours and that responds more effectively and efficiently to students' needs, especially when integrated with other student-centered approaches and models of instruction. Let's look at how RTI integrates with a PLC, IB PYP, and personalized learning.

RTI, PLC, PYP, and Personalized Learning

RTI complements the PLC process, the IB PYP framework, and personalized learning to maximize student achievement in schools. As part of the PLC process, collaborative grade-level, subject, or transdisciplinary teams meet regularly to ask and answer the four critical questions focused on student learning (DuFour et al., 2016). After establishing a guaranteed and viable curriculum with identified essential standards (see chapter 1, page 13, and chapter 2, page 21, for more information on these processes), collaborative teams assess student understanding and realize some students have not yet mastered the essential curriculum, whereas other students have. This is when teams focus on the third and fourth PLC critical questions:

> How will we respond when some students don't learn?
>
> . . . How will we extend the learning for students who are already proficient? (DuFour et al., 2016, p. 36)

Regarding these questions, a collaborative teacher team will achieve the most gains by using RTI to address the essential skill deficits of and extension opportunities for learners. Likewise, the school leadership team can support grade-level collaborative teams by using another multitiered system of supports (such as School-Wide Positive Behavioral Supports or SWPBS; https://pbis.org/topics/school-wide) to support the identified, essential academic and social behaviors of learners. Coauthors Richard DuFour, Rebecca DuFour, Robert Eaker, Mike Mattos, and Anthony Muhammad (2021) provide a list of how a PLC (made up of many collaborative teams) can effectively answer critical questions three and four:

1. Create a master schedule that ensures all students have access to grade-level essential curricula and discontinue tracks of below-grade-level instruction.

2. Make sure the master schedule allows for additional support (Tiers 2 and 3) without the student missing new essential core instruction.

3. Embed the extra time and support during the regular school day.

4. Create a systematic intervention process.

5. Respond quickly and proactively when possible.

6. Target students for intervention by need and assign staff based on who is best trained.

7. Make interventions required.

8. Work together with staff to identify and teach essential behaviors (as part of core instruction).

9. Have a plan to extend student learning.

10. Do not deny students access to enrichment.

11. Ensure that schoolwide grading practices align with the outcome of giving students extra opportunities to demonstrate mastery of essential curricula.

12. Develop productive home partnerships, but don't make the intervention system dependent on parent and guardian participation. (pp. 203–205)

As mentioned previously, the school's leadership team plays an essential role in ensuring the school implements RTI with fidelity. Beyond that, collaborative teacher teams have a great responsibility and opportunity to know their students and guarantee success for all. Following is an example of how one fourth-grade collaborative team at the International Community School (ICS) of Addis Ababa worked together to ensure all students were learning at high levels.

Within the first two weeks of school, the grade 4 team had developed and committed to *team norms*: "ground rules or habits that govern the group" (DuFour et al.,

2016, p. 72). These norms were mostly based on the seven norms of collaboration (Garmston & Wellman, 2016) and the four PLC critical questions (DuFour et al., 2016). However, team norms were also individualized to the team, which agreed that ordering snacks from the campus canteen was a priority for Wednesday meetings. The leadership team was involved in identifying a grade 4 team leader, who acted as the liaison between the leadership team and the grade-level team. The leadership team also set the assessment schedule, the meeting agendas for all grade levels, and the master schedule (see figure 4.4, page 70). The grade 4 team met for forty-five minutes to an hour each day (when students went to their enrichment classes), and the IB PYP coordinator came to its collaborative team meetings two to three times per week. The team invited administrators and counselors to its meetings as needed. Leaders assigned a learning support teacher to the team, who participated in most planning meetings, as well as taught differentiated groups or co-taught with a classroom teacher. Leaders also assigned a specialist teacher to the team to facilitate interdisciplinary planning with enrichment, and he would come to collaborative team meetings once per week. Teachers typically had thirty to forty minutes to plan independently or in pairs based on what members discussed in the collaborative team meeting that day.

Once team norms were established and classroom routines and procedures were taught and practiced the first two weeks, the grade 4 team worked collaboratively, using the first two PLC critical questions as a guide to identify and collect the data members needed as they delved into building the learning community of grade 4 students. They began collecting reading (from the *Developmental Reading Assessment*, Second Edition [DRA-2]) and conferring data, writing samples, and number-readiness data (which included previous years' skills). This information helped the team identify intervention and extension groups, which would help members answer PLC critical questions three and four. These initial groups were meant to help prepare students for small-group learning and to help fill gaps that would prepare students for the first units of instruction. The intervention and extension groups took place during *grow time*, a thirty-minute dedicated block of time in the schedule to help students focus on personal areas of growth. More specifically, this dedicated time for Tier 2 support was highly aligned with the grade 4 standards and units of instruction. The goals for each group were very targeted, including the extension-group goals, for which students took the lead in setting their targets. Classroom teachers, educational assistants, the EAL teacher, and the learning support teacher were each teaching a small group during grow time.

Sample Elementary Schedule With Grow Time

	7:30–8:00 a.m.	8:00–8:30 a.m.	8:30–8:45 a.m.	8:45–9:00 a.m.	9:00–9:15 a.m.	9:15–9:30 a.m.	9:30–9:45 a.m.	9:45–10:00 a.m.	10:00–10:15 a.m.	10:15–10:30 a.m.	10:30–10:45 a.m.	10:45–11:00 a.m.	11:00–11:15 a.m.	11:15–11:30 a.m.
EY2													Movement (including transition)	
EY3		MM			Movement (including transition)									
EY4	Outdoor Learning Time With Specials/Prep EY 4/5 PG													
EY5		Morning Meeting					Grow Time		EY5 Snack EY 4/5 PG		Transition	Specials Prep		
Grade 1			Specials Collaborative Team Time				Gr 1 Snack LESPG						Grow Time	
Grade 2			Specials Collaborative Team Time			Specials Prep			Gr 2 Eat and Play LESPG	Grow Time 10:25–10:55 a.m.				
Grade 3								Gr 3 Eat and Play UESPG		Grow Time		Specials Collaborative Team Time		
Grade 4				Grow Time			Grade 4 Play and Eat UESPG							
Grade 5			Specials Prep		Specials Collaborative Team Time				Grade 5 Snack UES/PG					
Specialists	Specialists on Game Duty	Specialists Prep	Grade 2 Grade 5			Grade 2 Grade 5			Prep or Collaborative Team Time			EY5 Grade 3		

	11:30–11:45 a.m.	11:45 a.m.–12:00 p.m.	12:00–12:15 p.m.	12:15–12:30 p.m.	12:30–12:45 p.m.	12:45–1:00 p.m.	1:00–1:15 p.m.	1:15–1:30 p.m.	1:30–1:45 p.m.	1:45–2:00 p.m.	2:00–2:15 p.m.	2:15–2:30 p.m.	2:30–2:45 p.m.	2:45–3:00 p.m.	3:00–3:10 p.m.	3:10–3:20 p.m.
							Transition →								Dismissal →	
EY2		DS														
EY3	DS	DS	Lunch													
EY4			Lunch	Art or Gardening EY 4/5 PG Collaborative Team Time 1–2 p.m.												
EY5	Specials PLC			Lunch Cafeteria 12:15–12:35 LESPG 12:40–1:00 p.m. Flex												
Grade 1	Lunch Cafeteria 11:30–11:50 a.m. Recess LESPG 11:55 a.m.–12:15 p.m.								Specials Collaborative Team Time or Prep							
Grade 2				Recess LESPG 12:15–12:35 p.m. Lunch Cafeteria 12:40–1:00 p.m.												
Grade 3	Specials Prep			Lunch Roof 12:15–12:35 p.m. Recess UESPG 12:40–1:00 p.m. Flex												
Grade 4	Lunch Cafeteria Tents 11:30–11:50 a.m. Recess UESPG 11:55 a.m.–12:15 p.m.								Specials Collaborative Team Time or Prep							
Grade 5	Recess UES/PG 11:30–11:50 a.m. Lunch Cafeteria Tents 11:55 a.m.–12:15 p.m.						Grow Time									
Specialists	EY5 Grade 3			Lunch			Prep		Grade 1 Grade 4							

FIGURE 4.4: Sample elementary schedule with grow time.

DS: Dismissal; EY: Early years; LESPG: Lower elementary school playground; LE: Lower elementary; UE: Upper elementary; UESPG: Upper elementary school playground; MM: Morning meeting; PG: Playground; UE: Upper elementary; UESPG: Upper elementary school playground.

Source: © 2021 by the International Community School of Addis Ababa. Adapted with permission.

The teachers knew they would be directing this more at the beginning of the school year, with the plan to gradually release responsibility to students for planning their areas of growth as they were ready and as the year progressed. Each teacher used a goal-setting form, like the one in figure 4.5, to help students begin reflecting and taking some ownership of their learning.

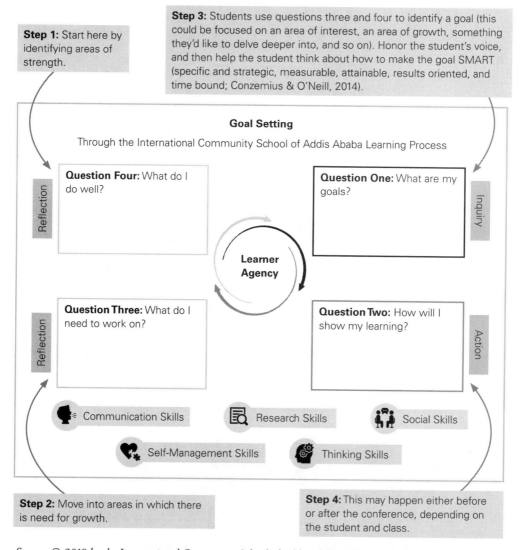

Step 1: Start here by identifying areas of strength.

Step 3: Students use questions three and four to identify a goal (this could be focused on an area of interest, an area of growth, something they'd like to delve deeper into, and so on). Honor the student's voice, and then help the student think about how to make the goal SMART (specific and strategic, measurable, attainable, results oriented, and time bound; Conzemius & O'Neill, 2014).

Goal Setting

Through the International Community School of Addis Ababa Learning Process

Reflection

Question Four: What do I do well?

Inquiry

Question One: What are my goals?

Learner Agency

Reflection

Question Three: What do I need to work on?

Action

Question Two: How will I show my learning?

Communication Skills   Research Skills   Social Skills

Self-Management Skills   Thinking Skills

Step 2: Move into areas in which there is need for growth.

Step 4: This may happen either before or after the conference, depending on the student and class.

Source: © 2019 by the International Community School of Addis Ababa. Adapted with permission.

FIGURE 4.5: Goal setting through the learning process example.

After four weeks, the grade 4 team members had started their units of instruction, and each of the four classroom teachers took the lead in planning a specific subject area, usually in collaboration with another teacher, educational assistant, or the PYP coordinator. Team members shared plans and resources using Google Drive docs and the learning management system the elementary school uses. During collaborative meetings, all team members discussed ideas and plans several team members had already mapped out prior to the meeting. Members drafted common formative assessments outside team meetings and reviewed them during team meetings. Using common formative assessment data of grade 4 standards, the team planned minilessons targeted for smaller groups of students based on their needs. This meant large-group instruction was very minimal throughout the day. The small groups were flexible and changed every few weeks, especially in mathematics. Before launching each unit of inquiry, teachers took a half-day planning retreat with the PYP coordinator to map out the essential concepts, standards, and skills (answering PLC critical question one) and some of the learning experiences and assessments (answering critical question two) that would guide student learning. Then, the team used one collaborative team meeting each week to further develop student learning experiences and assessments, and to analyze and respond to data. Reteaching and intervention focused on the missing knowledge and skills section of the critical question one document the team created for each unit (see an example in figure 4.6, page 74). These interventions were built into the instructional day, and they were sometimes addressed during grow time groups.

As the year progressed, teachers created a fluid system of personalized workshops focused on different essential skills or concepts being taught in each unit. They started the workshops after collecting some initial assessments and after providing students some instruction about the big ideas of the unit. Teachers used the already scheduled literacy, mathematics, and inquiry times to deliver the workshops. Students who demonstrated more independence in their learning could sign up for different workshops throughout the day or create their own personal inquiry plans if they demonstrated proficiency in the essential grade-level standards being taught. Teachers asked some student "experts" to lead workshops alongside the adults. Adults guided students who struggled with independence, and the teachers assigned these students to the workshops that supported their learning. These struggling students still had agency over how they demonstrated some of their learning, and teachers taught them to set and reflect on goals to build more skills for independence. Toward the end of each unit of inquiry, teachers gave students choice boards that allowed them to choose a pathway to demonstrate their understanding of key concepts and lines of inquiry.

How We Organize Ourselves (Grade 4) (Coggle link)		
• Central Idea: Systems can help communities and individuals respond to needs. • Lines of Inquiry: The impact of systems on a community (causation), our responsibility in systems (responsibility), ways decisions are made (causation)		
PLC Critical Question One: What do we want all students to know, understand, and be able to do?		
Understand (Conceptual Understandings)		
• Communities evaluate effectiveness of systems. • Individuals (and groups) recognize needs and develop an organization system to overcome challenges. • Individuals have a responsibility within their community. • There are different ways a decision can be made within a group.		
Know (Knowledge required to access the central idea)	**Do (Skills, ATLs)**	**Be (Dispositions; learner profile and traits)**

Understand how systems work (interacting parts; natural and then human made):
 	
• System—Interrelated parts working together (body systems, car engine, sports teams, school, restaurant, transportation, airports, library) to achieve a certain outcome
• Types of organizational systems:
  • Personal—Personal organization such as belongings, schedule of the day, technology, book box, and notebooks
  • Community—Drills at school, recess equipment, classroom jobs and committees, cafeteria, and library
  • Government—The way decisions are made depends on the type of government.
  • Roles, rights, and responsibilities within systems (connects to yearlong unit)
	Self-management skills:
	
	• Delegate and share responsibility for decision making.
	• Plan short- and long-term tasks.
	• Take on and complete tasks as agreed on.
	• Use technology effectively and productively.
	• Use time effectively and appropriately.
	
	Social skills:
	
	• Build consensus and negotiate effectively.
	• Take on a variety of roles in group learning.
	• Make fair and equitable decisions.
	• Be aware of own and others' impact as a member of a learning group.
	
	Other skills:
	
	• Use of a personal organization system and evaluation of its effectiveness
	• How to recognize needs
	• How to evaluate a system
	• How to evaluate own participation in a human-made system
		Growth mindset (connects to yearlong unit):
		
		• Principled
		• Reflective
		• Open-minded

Source: © 2020 by the International Community School of Addis Ababa. Adapted with permission.

FIGURE 4.6: How we organize ourselves (grade 4).

*Visit **go.SolutionTree.com/PLCbooks** for a free reproducible version of this figure.*

Later in the year, teachers gave students the opportunity to use the approaches to learning and learner profile traits from the IB PYP curriculum, as well as the instruction on goal setting and a learning process (that involved inquiry, action, and reflection) to plan their own personalized learning experience for one of the units of inquiry. Some students received extra adult support throughout the learning experience as needed. This experience turned out to be highly useful in helping students see the impact of their learning and hard work.

Every other week throughout the school year, the team met to address PLC critical questions three and four meetings (called *Q3/Q4 meetings*). The team also discussed questions three and four any time they reviewed data in meetings (which was frequently), but intentionally scheduled the Q3/Q4 meetings to review intervention group data and to have problem-solving discussions about specific students. See figure 4.7 and figure 4.8, page 78, for examples of protocols the team used in these meetings. (See the appendix to this chapter beginning on page 92 for an example of a completed problem-solving form [figures A.1 to A.5].)

Question Three and Question Four: Selecting or Reviewing Grow Time Interventions and Progress-Monitoring Tools Protocol, 2021–2022

Goals

Maintain a solution-focused, strengths-based approach to timely and efficient discussion of interventions and extensions.

Develop mutual accountability for maintaining these goals.

Key Features of This Protocol

1. Mutual accountability: All team members, not just the facilitator, are responsible to remind one another of the guidelines of the protocol. Pay attention to yourself and others.

2. Timekeeping and aim: All team members will adhere to the timing guidelines and the aim of each round of discussion to keep the session moving forward.

3. Reflection: At the end of each session, team members will self-evaluate their work according to the outcomes and the guidelines of the protocol. Were we effective, solution focused, and strengths based? What could we do better next time? Teams too busy to reflect are too busy to grow.

4. Documentation: Grade 4 teachers will document meetings, strategies, interventions, and next steps on the problem-solving form.

Source: © 2020 by the International Community School of Addis Ababa. Adapted with permission.

FIGURE 4.7: Questions three and four for selecting or reviewing grow time interventions and progress-monitoring tools protocol, 2021–2022.

continued →

Timing	Actions	Aims	Notes
Ahead of meeting time	• Choose area of focus (mathematics, reading, writing) and assign who will lead the gathering of data for which students. • Gather data and make them visually accessible to the team (tables, graphs, shared docs like this one). • Invite appropriate collaborators, such as speech-language pathologist, occupational therapist, English as an additional language (EAL) teacher, counselor, designated learning support personnel, and specialist representative.	Use data to guide the intervention goals and progress-monitoring tools for groups of students.	It's essential to bring data to these meetings and to make those data accessible to all stakeholders. All team members should review the data prior to the Q3/Q4 meeting.
Three minutes	Everyone looks at data. Round-robin share of one observation. Avoid evaluative causes, like "It looks like Emma was never taught phonics." No repeats.	Identify patterns or trends in the data. Prepare to create learning targets and identifying interventions and progress-monitoring tools.	This is a warm-up activity to get all stakeholders involved and thinking about the data.
Four minutes	Optional: If necessary, discuss if it would be helpful to collect more data to pinpoint specific areas for student growth.	Ensure the data are sufficient for making informed decisions about student areas of growth. Decide if and when to give further assessments.	Make or reshuffle grow time groups with the intention of collecting more data and sharing out at the next Q3/Q4 meeting.
Ten minutes	Classroom teachers take turns discussing and prioritizing the essential learning targets that students have or have not mastered based on the data.	Classroom teachers (curriculum experts) begin to identify possible grow time learning targets based on essential standards.	The learning support teacher will begin to draft possible grow time groups in a shared document as teachers are discussing and prioritizing the learning targets.
Three minutes	Review draft of grow time groups the LS teacher created and targets for each group.	Clearly identify adults and learning targets by each group. If time, discuss the location of these groups.	Try to match adults with groups based on areas of expertise and student rapport. If there's no time to discuss the location of these groups, this can be sorted after the meeting.

Three to five minutes	Decide which intervention best matches the learning targets for each group.	Ensure the team chooses the best interventions for the identified learning targets.	This document may be helpful in identifying available interventions.
Ten minutes	Discuss frequency of these groups and how each will collect and report data.	Identify the intensity of the intervention and the progress-monitoring tool to use.	Make sure the progress-monitoring tool matches and measures the identified learning target. Here are some ideas for progress-monitoring tools: • easyCBM (https://easycbm.com) measures • Developmental Reading Assessment/PMs • LLI Running Records • Timed writing samples (score based on learning target) • Some online programs have built in progress-tracking tools. • Mad minutes (mathematics facts) or Eureka sprints • Exit tickets (percentage of accuracy or scaled 1–4) • Rubrics or checklists
Total: Thirty to thirty-five minutes per subject area			
Afterward	Learning support teacher helps gather any materials or tools that can support grow time groups. If a location was not determined for each group, the learning support teacher can help make that determination and add this in a shared document or the daily slides.	Make sure everyone is ready and equipped to work with their grow time group.	Idea: It may help to create a document that limits the student names, learning targets, and resources for each grow time group (for organizing, recording, reporting, and substitute plan purposes).

Question Three and Question Four: Initial Student-Discussion Protocol, 2021–2022

Goals

Maintain a solution-focused, strengths-based approach to timely and efficient discussion of students of concern.

Develop mutual accountability for maintaining these goals.

Key Features of This Protocol

1. Mutual accountability: All team members, not just a facilitator, are responsible to remind one another of the protocol guidelines. Pay attention to self and others.

2. Timekeeping and aim: All team members will adhere to the timing guidelines and the aim of each round of discussion to keep the session moving forward.

3. Reflection: At the end of each session, team members will self-evaluate their work according to the protocol outcomes and the guidelines. Were we effective, solution-focused, and strengths-based? What could we do better next time? Teams who are too busy to reflect are too busy to grow.

4. Documentation: Grade 4 teachers will document meetings, strategies, interventions, and next steps on the problem-solving form.

Timing	Actions	Aims	Notes
Ahead of time	Nominate student by adding to agenda before student services team meeting. Invite appropriate collaborators—for example, speech-language pathologist, occupational therapist, English as an additional language teacher, counselor, designated learning support personnel, and specialist representative.	Be ready to have the most effective conversation possible about a student.	It's essential for students to be on the list ahead of time so the team can prepare to discuss them effectively. While occasionally students will be added, best practice is to prepare ahead.
One minute	Share positive information in round robins. No repeats! Use a signal for a repeat.	Identify strengths, assets, or learning profile traits in areas of success for the student.	Share an authentic strength. It's not necessary for every teacher to share just to "say something nice." Learner profile traits are an excellent place to start (for example, principled, caring, thinker, open-minded, knowledgeable, balanced, courageous, reflective, inquirer, communicator).
Two minutes	Optional: If available, share brief historical data.	Highlight any pertinent documentation from previous years.	Avoid unnecessary information.
One minute	Teacher who nominated the student shares challenges and concerns.	Provide clear statements of concern.	Share facts and nonjudgmental feedback as much as possible in this section.

Two minutes	Other teachers share their concerns. No repeats! Use a signal for a repeat.	Look for patterns.	Avoid negativity with the issues put forward.
One minute	Nominating teachers share interventions they have tried.	Provide examples of effective and noneffective interventions.	Keep the conversation focused on solutions. Give clear examples from the list of interventions.
Three minutes	Other teachers share their interventions, with an emphasis on interventions that *did* work.	Provide more examples of effective interventions.	Make clear examples from the effective interventions.
Three minutes	Optional: In the absence of good solutions emerging, use brainstorming. In collaboration, pairs of team members write on sticky notes a suggested intervention, then share.	Share crowd sourcing suggested interventions.	Document all suggestions for possible later use.
One minute	Nominating teachers commit to trying at least one suggested intervention for a two-week time period.	Have a solution focus and commitment.	Nominating teachers commit to making a plan of intervention for two weeks. Consider how you will set yourself up for success in implementing this intervention. What support might you need? How will you monitor the success or failure of the intervention? How will you ensure it doesn't go by the wayside? How will you remember to document this intervention on the problem-solving form?
One minute	Learning support representative confirms students to discuss in two weeks and adds to the appropriate agenda.	Systematize the follow-up.	If successful, the nominating teachers might only add positive notes to the agenda. If unsuccessful, ensure the team maintains focus and follows up with students of concern.

Source: © 2020 by the International Community School of Addis Ababa. Adapted with permission.

FIGURE 4.8: Question three and question four initial student-discussion protocol, 2021–2022.

continued ➡

Total: Fifteen minutes per student			
Afterward	Learning support representative communicates the intervention plan to all the student's teachers.	Standardize expectations for intervention and opportunities for student success.	Idea: Learning support representative considers adding calendar invites for teachers to update the problem-solving form on a weekly basis after this meeting.

In these meetings, members brought data (or had inputted the date into spreadsheets beforehand) for small grade 4 learning community groups. During these meetings, leaders reviewed and sometimes adjusted grow time (intervention and extension) groups. Members discussed individual students and initiated problem-solving forms for students showing significant struggles in any area. The team developed and implemented new interventions, reviewing them every four to six weeks. If a student was not responding to an intervention, the grade 4 team referred the student to a *student focus team* of administrators, counselors, a school psychologist, learning specialists, and the classroom teacher. This team developed an action plan (see figure 4.9) they followed up on after a few weeks. Many of the students in grade 4 began to make expected progress, while others continued to need other interventions and more intensive support and were eventually put on individualized learning plans (ILPs). The grade 4 learning support teacher oversaw coordinating the services of students on ILPs, as well as monitoring and supporting grow time interventions and extensions. This teacher ensured students with the highest needs were receiving all tiers of instruction to be successful. She would strategically pull students who needed Tier 3 support during a time when they were not missing other critical instruction. Usually, these students were pulled during independent work time to receive intensive intervention on the foundational skills they were missing.

One great advantage the grade 4 team had in facilitating collaboration and flexible learning options for students was how the classroom was set up. The classroom was a large, hub-style learning environment in which four classroom teachers and four educational assistants supported between seventy-five and eighty-five students. The classroom was in a large space with flexible seating, breakout rooms, and various types of quieter and noisier learning spaces. The variety in learning spaces and seating options allows teachers to be creative and flexible in teaching small groups of students. Even outdoor spaces were set up in a way that supported learning. Students helped to reimagine and redesign the space as part of their first inquiry unit to meet their learning needs. Breakout rooms were reserved throughout the day for groups and individual students who needed a quieter, less distracting place for learning.

Section B: Plan of Action and Implementation		
Plan of Action		
Through implementation of interventions in the Tier 1 setting, a targeted evidence-based plan of action is developed to implement in the classes where the teacher noted this student need. It is important to collaborate on developing the plan so the teachers can share global concerns and successful teaching strategies and interventions. Each teacher implementing the plan of action should use the intervention log to record the interventions and note their effectiveness. Share this information with the team when it reviews the plan of action.		
Plan of Action **(Add this student back to the Q3/Q4 agenda after two weeks.)**	**Persons Responsible** **(Include other support personnel: learning coach, principals, counselors, and so on.)**	**Start Date**
Continue interventions and start progress monitoring. Do a behavior observation looking at independence, processing time, and executive functioning behaviors.	Grade 4 adults Abe (student)	October 15 Week of October 19
Create a work basket of tasks for the student to do independently, conduct a classroom observation, set up a parent meeting, continue to collect data, include the student in a peer social skills group during lunch with the counselors, and meet back in two weeks. Schedule Tier 3 interventions for the student, coordinate EAL and Tier 3 interventions so they are fluid and complementary, develop executive functioning and social skills interventions, and communicate these with the team; update progress monitoring, plan of action, and parent communication section in the problem-solving form.	Grade 4 teachers, counselors, and the principal Grade 4 teachers, learning support teacher, EAL teacher, counselors	Week of November 2 November 13

Source: © 2020 by the International Community School of Addis Ababa. Adapted with permission.

FIGURE 4.9: Plan of action and implementation.

*Visit **go.SolutionTree.com/PLCbooks** for a free reproducible version of this figure.*

The EAL specialist and learning support teacher often used these rooms to work with students in need of Tier 3 instruction. Challenges to the hub learning environment occurred for some students who required less stimulation and noise to learn, and accommodations were put in place for those students. Overall, the grade 4 team worked collaboratively to ensure all students and teachers had a designated space to teach and learn throughout the school day.

The work of the grade 4 team highlights initial steps schools can take to make teaching and learning more collaborative, transferable, systematic, personalized, and thus more highly effective. The following section provides more detail on specific actions the grade 4 team took to create a highly successful learning environment.

Committing to Norms and Focusing on the PLC Questions

The priority for the grade 4 team was to commit to team norms, which included committing to the PLC process and taking collective responsibility for the learning of all students. Next, the team decided on the essential skills to assess to screen for learning gaps before launching the grade 4 units of instruction. They used screening data on universal skills to help students get the support they needed early in the school year. The learning support teacher and EAL specialists helped the classroom teachers and educational assistants gather some of these data. To respond most effectively to intensive learning needs, the team gathered the screening data from the previous school year so intensive interventions could start as soon as possible. In schools with high turnover, some of the data gathering would take place as new students are admitted. The admissions team can also gather some of these data.

Leaders designed the schedule and staffing to start both intensive and targeted interventions within the first month of school, and the team met weekly at the beginning of the school year to make decisions and respond to students' academic needs. The team also met regularly to decide the essential literacy, mathematics, and IB PYP conceptual understandings and skills for each unit (PLC critical question one) and to create or review common formative assessments (PLC critical question two) that would guide decisions regarding intervention and extension (PLC critical questions three and four). The grade 4 team committed to asking and answering the critical questions during *every* collaborative planning meeting.

Developing Effective Planning and Teaching Strategies

It's clear that collaborative and efficient planning is a hallmark of the grade 4 team. Team members worked hard to create a high level of trust and collaboration from the beginning of the school year. This does not mean there were no conflicts on the team; members experienced a fair amount of conflict, but their commitments and accountability to team norms helped them remain productive. The team met each day, focusing on a different subject area while keeping in mind that all subject areas connect to transdisciplinary themes or conceptual, transferable learning. As the year progressed, the team members developed clearer priorities, well-defined roles and responsibilities, and decision-making rules that enhanced their productivity. The team members learned to have razor-sharp clarity on what was most important for student learning and focused all their efforts on those actions. This relates to what Hattie (2012) describes as collective teacher efficacy, which can happen best in the context of a PLC.

With the help of the school leadership team, the grade 4 team leader used effective leadership strategies to respond to the needs of her team, offering more support and direction when members needed it, and moving toward delegation as much as possible when everyone was on the same page. The team used a clear agenda, aligned with the team's commitments, in every meeting. The team members learned to maximize their planning time by occasionally using some of the team time to split up and focus on planning different areas of the curriculum, and then coming back together to review what they accomplished or decide the next steps. The team frequently collected and analyzed common formative assessment data, which made learning engagements more effective. When it became clear that some team members were more experienced with effective teaching approaches in an area, those team members would help share their expertise with the rest of the team. For example, two teachers on the team were highly skilled in utilizing a workshop approach to improve students' literacy skills. The team developed and implemented a lab site protocol to help all team members (including educational assistants) learn how to effectively confer with students to improve their learning. The other team members were able to watch the highly skilled teachers confer with students, and then they were able to try the same strategies immediately and receive feedback.

In addition to effective collaboration during team meetings and the decision to observe and learn from one another, the team created shared online planning sheets and slides (see figure 4.10, page 84), which allowed them to plan and communicate more efficiently. Team members became adept at using technology and a variety of resources to facilitate their own and students' learning. Collaborating with the EAL specialist, learning support teacher, and other specialists helped the team to utilize the most effective teaching strategies and supports to help all students learn at high levels. Sometimes this took the form of consultation, while other times the team utilized co-planning or co-teaching methods. The learning support teacher took the lead on directing and supporting grow time interventions and extensions in collaboration with the grade 4 team. Administrators and learning coaches were highly involved in supporting the team, often assisting in creating critical question one documents, sorting data, and procuring resources. This shows that when collaboration is done well, in the context of a PLC at Work, it elevates the learning of all members who learn together in the hub.

Grade 4 Hub Planning, 2022–2023					
	Monday October 4	Tuesday October 5	Wednesday October 6	Thursday October 7	Friday October 8
8:00 a.m.	Morning Meeting				
	SEL connections in small groups	Editing conventions and open house	Unit of inquiry connection	Mathematics (number talk, puzzle, routine) safe haven drill	Team-building game
			Wellness choices (8:20 a.m.)		
			Track		
8:30 a.m.	Grow time		Just dance	Grow time	
	Literacy groups	Literacy groups	Nature walk	Mathematics groups	Mathematics groups
			Jump rope		
			Basketball		
			Gardening		
9:00 a.m.	Independent writing	Independent reading	Centers	Independent writing	Independent writing
9:30 a.m.	Snack at hardtop	Snack at playground	Digital reading notebook Word inquiry Partner writing Toddle (www.toddleapp.com) learning journey Unit of inquiry and IXL (www. ixl.com) diagnostic	Snack at hardtop	Snack at playground
10:00 a.m.	Mathematics workshop	Mathematics workshop	Snack and recess at hardtop (10:10–10:40 a.m.)	Mathematics workshop	Mathematics centers
		Group one: Link learning target with resources and assigned teachers. Start with number talk (no more than ten minutes). Minilesson: Model and teach with the application problem (seven minutes). Practice (twenty minutes) Reflect and share (three minutes).			Potential games or centers: Comparing numbers (3, 4, 5, 6 digits) Addition and subtraction war Race to 100 and 1,000 Place value word problems Marcy Cook multiplication

Source: © 2021 by the International Community School of Addis Ababa. Adapted with permission.

FIGURE 4.10: Grade 4 hub planning, 2022–2023.

Creating a Systematic Intervention Process

The focus of this chapter is on developing a systematic intervention process. According to DuFour and colleagues (2021), this process is composed of six steps:

1. Identify students who need intervention.
2. Target the right intervention to meet each need.
3. Determine which staff members or members are best trained to meet each need.
4. Monitor each student's progress to determine whether the intervention is working.
5. Revise if a student is not responding to the intervention.
6. Extend learning once a student has mastered the essential curriculum. (p. 213)

The grade 4 team example illustrates how a collaborative team can complete these steps. First, the team members identified the essential knowledge and skills that would allow their grade 4 students to access the first units of instruction. Also, using screening data and assistance from the EAL and learning support teachers, they were able to identify students in need of intensive interventions. After that, they thoughtfully organized interventions and extensions; interventions were not optional for students.

The schedule was set up to allow for core, supplemental, and intensive interventions. Teachers also had plenty of collaborative time built into the schedule, as well as a dedicated time for reviewing data, individual students, and intervention and extension groups (Q3/Q4 meetings every other week). Tier 2 interventions happened during grow time, and Tier 3 interventions were organized during a time outside Tier 1 and Tier 2 instruction and not during enrichment. The EAL teacher would pull some students from their extra world languages class to develop their English skills before adding a third or additional language. Tier 2 interventions were re-evaluated every four to six weeks, and the intervention and extension groups became fluid and dynamic. Once members identified knowledge and skill gaps, adults would meet with students to help them understand the gap and create both a sense of urgency and hope. The adults worked with students to help them set goals and learn the essential skills to help them be successful in Tier 1. Because the team clearly identified the Tier 1 essential skills at the start of each unit (eventually this became easier for teacher teams each year, due to the records and plans recorded in the learning management system), the team had an efficient way to create assessments and identify students in need of supplemental intervention or extension.

Once Tier 2 interventions started and the team created and adjusted groups, it became manageable for the grade 4 team to focus on the targeted goals and track data for a smaller number of students. Teachers, educational assistants, and specialists were all part of delivering interventions and extensions and collecting data. These adults started problem-solving forms for students who showed a consistent need for Tier 2 support in multiple subjects or over the course of a couple of months or units. This started the necessary documentation trail that would support the decision to bring up a student for review to another collaborative school team called the *student focus team*.

When it became clear grade 4 students were not responding to multiple intervention attempts, they were systematically brought up to the student focus team to get further expertise and resources to support the students' learning. Sometimes this meant the student focus team trying yet a different intervention or increasing the intensity of an intervention. Other times, the student focus team made a referral for testing if a student's profile warranted it, and if the team needed more information regarding how that student learns or processes information. Regardless of the outcome of the student focus team meeting, students each had multiple sets of expert eyes collectively taking responsibility for their learning at high levels. Occasionally, the student focus team would bring up students in a meeting without having to go through all the Tier 2 interventions and documentation in the classroom first. The student focus team made this decision on a case-by-case basis, and it was usually the result of a student whose behavior, attendance, or academic performance was so concerning that intensive or additional support was immediately necessary for that student to be successful. Once the student focus team determined a student needed intensive support to be successful, the team placed the student on an individualized learning plan. Parents were always involved at this step, and they were encouraged to understand and support the learning goals the team developed specifically for their children.

It's important to note that the person most highly qualified and trained in that area of need should develop and implement the intensive learning plans. For example, the EAL teacher should be the one to create a targeted EAL plan and deliver instruction on those goals at the most appropriate time. A counselor will help to develop and implement a positive behavior support plan for a student with intensive behavior needs. A learning support or special education teacher will develop and implement an individualized learning plan for students with intensive academic needs or learning gaps. The student focus team will collect data more frequently on these students, and the team reviews its plans and progress at regular intervals. The collaborative grade-level team shares collective responsibility for students receiving Tier 3 intervention and ensures members meet each student's accommodations and needs throughout the school day. When this happens, all students can learn at high levels and continue making progress.

Making Learning More Personalized

In addition to using highly effective approaches like RTI, the grade 4 team also employed learning-progressive approaches and incorporated the IB PYP's focus on student agency with a personalized learning approach. Specifically, the team leveraged the already scheduled grow time to introduce targeted learning goals and plans, with the intention of gradually releasing responsibility to students for planning or working on their own areas for growth. The team utilized goal-setting forms with the four PLC critical questions to help students start thinking of their learning in a systematic way and begin taking ownership over it. Teachers have students who demonstrated a need for extension of the grade 4 learning targets develop their own learning plans to further or deepen their understanding of the grade 4 skills or even to target higher-level skills. For example, a group of grade 4 readers needing extension met and discussed their interests as well as how they might deepen their understanding of the grade 4 literacy standards. They decided to form book clubs based on common interests, and, with the help of an adult, each small book club group decided which standards and reading behaviors to target, as well as how they would demonstrate and celebrate their learning when finished with their book. In this way, the team encouraged students to ask and answer the four PLC critical questions for themselves:

1. What do I want to know, understand, and be able to do?
2. How will I demonstrate that I have learned it?
3. What will I do when I am not learning?
4. What will I do when I have already learned it? (Stuart, Heckmann, Mattos, & Buffum, 2018, pp. 16–17)

The grade 4 teachers understood that putting the students at the center of their learning was the optimal state and would set students up for future success. At the same time, these teachers faced the reality that many students were not ready to take ownership of their learning, especially at the beginning of the school year. The teachers needed to create the space and opportunities for students to desire and accept this level of engagement and responsibility. One way teachers did this was to create a system of targeted workshops in which students could focus on an area of interest or needed development, and have students sign up for workshops throughout the learning blocks each day. For students who were not independent at determining their areas of needed development, or for students with major skill gaps (students in need of Tier 3 intervention), a teacher would often guide students in selecting their daily workshops. Still, teachers gave these students some choice and voice in how they demonstrated their learning and ownership of their learning (with frequent adult check-ins and accountability) after setting a daily learning goal.

Some students demonstrated they were experts in some grade 4 expectations, and teachers challenged them to teach a workshop alongside an adult. This helped in solidifying students' learning and taking that learning to a new level. It also helped to set an example for other young learners in what could be possible for them with enough time and effort. The admiration and recognition that went along with becoming an "expert" or teacher motivated many students. Teachers often gave students in need of extension the opportunity and challenge to lead in this way. This opportunity wasn't limited to a selective group of students, though. Grade 4 teachers looked for ways to have *every student* become an expert, a teacher of something throughout the school year. Units of inquiry offered teachers opportunities to find unique talents, background knowledge, and strengths among students who were not proficient in basic literacy or numeracy skills.

The unit of inquiry allowed for the most personalization in how students demonstrate their understanding of key concepts and skills. Toward the end of each unit, teachers offered learning choice boards, which gave students the option of a personalized pathway for demonstrating their understanding of key concepts and lines of inquiry. Teachers selected one unit of inquiry to turn into a personalized learning experience from the start of the unit. For a unit taught toward the end of the school year, adults offered varying levels of guidance to students throughout the unit. This allowed students to apply the skills they had been trying out and learning all year, and it became an empowering time for many young learners as they saw the impact of their hard work and personal learning process (involving inquiry, action, and reflection) on the community of learners and the community at large. Even if their impact was small, or they required much guidance, students were able to participate in real-world learning and reflect on their efforts and results.

Figure 4.11, from *Personalized Learning in a PLC at Work*, illustrates how RTI can integrate well into the context of a PLC and personalized learning school (Stuart et al., 2018). The previous examples from the grade 4 team illustrate how members implemented RTI within IB PYP's framework or transdisciplinary learning and units of inquiry. Altogether, these student-centered approaches make the greatest impact on student learning and success.

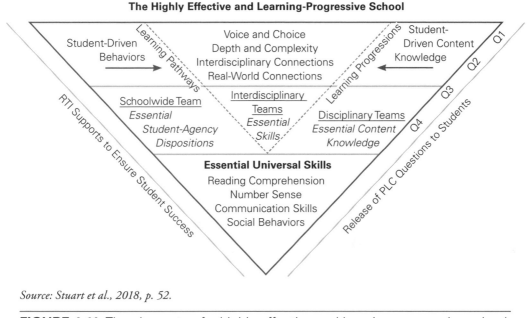

Source: Stuart et al., 2018, p. 52.

FIGURE 4.11: The elements of a highly effective and learning-progressive school.

Utilizing and Maximizing the Learning Space

One might argue that the grade 4 team's learning space allowed members to have such a collaborative, effective, and progressive learning atmosphere. It is true that a hub model of learning is the most flexible and collaborative, but it also poses a threat to student learning if members do not utilize the PLC process and student-centered teaching approaches. A hub learning environment is not the single most important factor for improving student learning, but this kind of environment enhances collaborative teaching and learning, and offers great flexibility to students and teachers. Still, even if a school is not intentionally built with learning hubs, there are actions teams can take to create a more collaborative and flexible learning environment, which will improve both teacher and student learning.

The grade 4 team took the following actions nearly any school team could take to maximize its learning spaces.

1.   Designate spaces for presentations where noisy and collaborative learning can take place.

2.   Designate spaces around the hub where students and teachers can go for quieter or more focused learning.

3.   Be creative and utilize every possible space, including outdoor learning spaces.

4.   As part of a comprehensive and intentional learning experience, involve students in reimagining and redesigning the classroom space to improve learning for all.

5.   Create and review a system to ensure teachers use the spaces in an equitable, organized manner and for their intended purpose: to maximize learning.

6.   Provide accommodations for students who require less environmental stimulation to learn.

Conclusion

In this chapter, I discussed how RTI is a complementary and necessary framework that supports the PLC process in helping all students learn at high levels, especially in the context of a school that uses other student-centered approaches and frameworks, such as the IB PYP and personalized learning. It is important for leaders to model collective responsibility and hire people who are willing to take collective responsibility for the learning of every student. The grade 4 example models this attitude. You learned from the grade 4 team how collaborative teacher teams can effectively use the schedule, collaborative team time, adult resources, a systematic intervention process, and a hub-style learning environment to maximize learning. All the pieces fit together when a school is functioning as a PLC at Work.

Next Steps

Consider the following suggested actions for getting started on becoming highly effective and then moving to the next level by becoming learning progressive.

Getting Started on Being Highly Effective

- Ensure a guiding coalition (or school leadership team) is in place and start there. This coalition should meet to determine whether the school's current practices support the adoption of an RTI model; if not, the team can use RTI checklists to establish goals and benchmarks for the effective implementation of RTI. Goals and objectives will likely include making RTI part of staff development and establishing some RTI experts at the school.

- Hire professionals who believe all students (who professionals expect to live independently one day) can learn at high levels, and who are likewise acting on this belief.

- Ensure an RTI expert is involved in conversations about PLC critical questions three and four.

Moving to the Next Level—Becoming Learning Progressive

- Reorganize the master schedule to support daily interventions and extensions as part of the norm of what to expect throughout the day. You could design blocks of time each day when no new critical instruction (core or Tier 1) is happening. Ensure teams use data effectively and learning targets are clear for interventions and extensions, and mandate the interventions.

- Ensure teams develop and utilize common formative assessments well and often, as these data are necessary for setting up targeted interventions and extensions. The leadership team (or guiding coalition) can create an accountability tool or conduct regular observations to support collaborative teams in their strategic use of common formative assessments. Collaborative teams should meet at least every other week to discuss PLC critical questions three and four, and systematically adjust or continue interventions and extensions as needed, based on data.

- Hand over the four PLC critical questions to students as you help them develop the skills to set their own learning targets, thus making interventions and extensions more personalized. Consider handing over this responsibility gradually, as students show they are ready. Be sure to give plenty of instruction and opportunities for students to have agency over different aspects of their learning.

 **Appendix**

The following figures in the chapter appendix represent a completed problem-solving form. Figure A.1 (page 93) is an individual student problem-solving form for Tiers 1 and 2. Figure A.2 (page 94) provides a brief summary of attempted intervention strategies. Figure A.3 (page 95) is a brief summary of parent contact. Figure A.4 (page 97) shows a progress-monitoring log, and figure A.5 (98) shows an interventions review.

Tiers 1 and 2: Individual Student Problem-Solving Form	
Section A: Relevant Student Data	
Student Name: Sample Student	Date: October 14, 2020
Referring Teacher: Ms. M. and grade-level team	Grade: 4

Student Strengths and Successes: (Please list.)

The student loves his family; he is always talking about them. He has a desire to please and do well. He wants to learn. He is quite funny (even if it's not always purposeful) and very kind to teachers.

State and describe the problem, and then attach relevant data: (If behavioral, include what happens before, during, and after.)

Student is unable to start, continue, or complete tasks in any subject area. He needs adult guidance in understanding directions. He also needs one-to-one support to produce any kind of writing.

He did not get any questions right on the beginning-of-the-year number-readiness assessment; teachers read and divided everything into individual steps on that assessment.

He is at Developmental Reading Assessment 3.

October 22, 2020, Phonics Screener Results:

- Capital letters—25/26 (missed /G/)
- Lowercase letters—25/26 (missed /g/)
- Consonant sounds—18/21 (missed /c/, /q/, /x/)
- Short vowel sounds—0/5
- CVC words—2/13
- Beginning blends—3/19
- Ending blends—2/9
- Beginning digraphs—4/14
- Ending digraphs—1/10

October 23, 2020 Phonemic Awareness Assessment:

Student demonstrated relative strengths in the following areas: single syllable onset-rhyme blending, syllable blending and pronouncing, phoneme isolation of initial sounds, and phoneme isolation of final sounds. He demonstrated weaknesses in the following areas: rhyme production, single-syllable onset-rhyme segmenting, syllable segmenting and counting, phoneme alliteration and discrimination, phoneme isolation of medial sounds, phoneme blending, phoneme addition, phoneme substitution, and phoneme deletion. On the assessment, the student kept asking the teacher for directions and to repeat words. He asked for more examples sometimes, but even with the examples, he was unable to transfer and perform the necessary skills. He seemed to be comfortable and paying attention during the assessment.

Student struggles to explain his thoughts in Amharic (native language) as well as English. He is nervous about making mistakes. He also struggles with understanding social situations.

(Link previous problem-solving forms here.)

Source: © 2021 by the International Community School of Addis Ababa. Adapted with permission.

FIGURE A.1: Tiers 1 and 2 individual student problem-solving form.

*Visit **go.SolutionTree.com/PLCbooks** for a free reproducible version of this figure.*

Brief Summary of Attempted Intervention Strategies

Note: The tiers 1 and 2 instructional strategies sheet is not only a work in progress but also a live document. Instructional coaches and all team members can add ideas to the form as they discuss strategies to meet student needs.

Interventions and Accommodations	Duration	Person Responsible	Outcome
EAL small group (reading sight words, listening and speaking: simple conversations, sharing stories, asking questions)	During French time (45 minutes every other day); started at the beginning of the school year	Mr. B.	Student enjoys the group and seems to be benefiting from the instruction; continue to monitor. After the first few weeks, sample student's behavior in the small group has deteriorated. He is often disruptive unless given one-to-one attention.
One-to-one writing support using word banks, sentence starters, visuals, and checklists for breaking down task	Daily as needed during journaling time and writer's workshop; started at the beginning of the school year	Adults in 4B	Student is not writing anything without direct and constant adult assistance; continue to monitor. As of October 23, sample student is sometimes able to start writing independently, if teacher gives one-to-one instructions and practices idea generation. Independent writing will continue for two to three minutes but is also inconsistent.
Two different small reading groups (in addition to EAL group)—phonics and decoding and comprehension	Decoding group, three times per week (begin October 12); phonics group, three times per week (began October 19)	Educational assistants with guidance from the learning support teacher	Student enjoys his decoding group and instruction, but he still requires prompting and teacher support to use any of the taught decoding strategies. Phonics group is too new to comment on.
Mathematics group, games to focus on number ID and one-to-one correspondence	When needed (began October 5)	Educational assistants with guidance from the learning support teacher	Will begin progress monitoring (using number-readiness assessment) during week of October 26
Prewriting strategy group	Three times per week (began October 12)	Educational assistants with guidance from the classroom teacher	Performance and retention are inconsistent.

Source: © 2021 by the International Community School of Addis Ababa. Adapted with permission.

FIGURE A.2: Brief summary of attempted intervention strategies.

Visit **go.SolutionTree.com/PLCbooks** for a free reproducible version of this figure.

Brief Summary of Parent Contact		
(Please include the date, who made the contact, the nature of the discussion, and any relevant information and <u>meeting minutes [link]</u>.)		
October 14: parent contact made by Ms. R., via email; checked on student's feelings after his first month at ICS and shared that sample student seems happy at school and is quite social; and also made parents aware student is not only receiving English support from Mr. B. but also academic interventions (small groups and one-to-one) in other subject areas.		
<u>Meeting minutes [link]</u>		
Any other pertinent information:		

Teacher	Details	Date
Mr. O.	Student is new to our school, and he is coming from the ABC schools system. He received average marks in all areas at his last school.	October 14
Ms. M.	Communication with student's parents was tricky at the beginning of the year. After three different teachers attempted to contact parents, Mrs. G. phoned the home and told parents they needed to respond to teacher emails in order for sample student to receive pull-out with Mr. B. I (Ms. M.) received email communication from sample student's older sister about a week later—she was sending photos for sample student's writing but then also asked for an update on how he was doing in class. She also asked if she could support in any way. Lines of communication within family are not quite clear.	
Mr. O.	Student said he did not learn to read or write in Amharic, even though he was instructed to read and write it at the Intellectual Schools. He said he lived in the United States for two years (but he didn't remember where) when he was four to six years old. He also said his mom has him read to her at home, and he also has a tutor he reads to.	October 23
Ms. V.	Observation notes	November 2 and 16
Ms. M.	Both parents are now in Dubai. Student is living with his cousins and maybe an uncle.	November 16
Ms. M.	Student will start meeting with an ICS tutor, two days per week for an hour-and-a-half each; tutor will communicate with Mr. O. about appropriate tasks and focus areas (to match what student is working on at school). Student will Zoom with his tutor over winter break.	December 16

Source: © 2021 by the International Community School of Addis Ababa. Adapted with permission.

FIGURE A.3: Brief summary of parent contact.

*Visit **go.SolutionTree.com/PLCbooks** for a free reproducible version of this figure.*

Section C: Progress Monitoring

Fill out and discuss during question three and four meetings.

Intervention	Data Points	Conclusion to Share With Team at Review
With what and how often will progress be monitored?	**Scan and upload copies into the student's folder if needed.**	
Intervention: Small-group phonics and decoding instruction—two or three sessions per day Progress monitor: Weekly letter-sound fluency probes	Dates and Data Points: Words Their Way Inventory September 20—consonants, 100 percent accurate; short vowels, 14 percent accurate November 13—consonants 100 percent accurate, short vowels 14 percent accurate (no growth) December 16—consonants 100 percent accurate, short vowels 14 percent accurate (no growth) Letter-sounding fluency probes (sixty seconds): October 27—29 correct November 3—57 correct November 6—54 correct November 18—47 correct *Although we count them as correct, sample student adds an "uh" to the end of each sound. November 23—70 correct November 25—58 correct November 30—75 correct December 4—36 correct December 7—68 correct December 16—35 correct Notes:	(Include how long the intervention was in place.) Phonics-specific intervention: four weeks Decoding and phonics intervention: eight weeks *Both groups ended on November 13 (see the following new phonics intervention). Performance is inconsistent.

Intervention: Small-group mathematics games focused on numeracy. Progress monitor: Select portions of number-readiness assessment.	Dates and Data Points: 10 frames fluency (thirty seconds) October 21—10 percent correct October 28—100 percent correct November 13—50 percent correct November 18—100 percent correct (only took twenty-nine seconds) Portion of number-readiness assessment October: 1/5 on number-sense questions November: 5/5 on number-sense questions	Mathematics intervention interrupted but seems to be working. Increase frequency?
	Notes:	
Intervention: One-to-one instruction focused on short and long vowel sounds, as well as CVC and CVCe patterns	Dates and Data Points: Baseline on November 13—Short vowels, 14 percent December 16—Short vowels, 14 percent (no growth) Notes:	No growth in short vowel sounds between September 20 and December 16. Ms. M. began working one-to-one with sample student at the beginning of November on this skill (four days per week, twenty minutes each). Mr. O. began working with sample student at the end of November for this skill (five days per week). Still no growth.

Source: © 2021 by the International Community School of Addis Ababa. Adapted with permission.

FIGURE A.4: Progress-monitoring log.

*Visit **go.SolutionTree.com/PLCbooks** for a free reproducible version of this figure.*

Section D: Interventions Review
Date of Meeting: November 12, 2020
Teachers Present:
Ms. M., Mr. L., Ms. V., Mr. B., Mr. O., Mrs. G., Mrs. C.
The team determines the intervention was:
☐ Successful; interventions will stop and teachers will monitor the student
☐ Somewhat working; interventions will continue; make parent contact (will continue some Tier 2 interventions)
☒ Not working; team will change interventions or request Tier 3 support; make parent contact.
This decision was made based on the following evidence.
Meeting with parents to learn more about student's developmental history and language abilities because student still needs a tremendous amount of adult assistance daily in the classroom, and he has been acting out more. Also, according to multiple assessments (Measures of Academic Progress [MAP], Developmental Reading Assessment, CWA, classroom assessments), he is still more than two years behind. He is not making adequate progress even with Tier 2 interventions.
Date and Summary of Parent Contact or Meeting Minutes (link):
ILP Meeting on December 1 (link); there was a delay because parents were in Dubai)

Source: © 2021 by the International Community School of Addis Ababa. Adapted with permission.

FIGURE A.5: Interventions review.

*Visit **go.SolutionTree.com/PLCbooks** for a free reproducible version of this figure.*

 # References and Resources

Batsche, G. M., Castillo, J. M., Dixon, D. N., & Forde, S. (2008). Best practices in designing, implementing and evaluating quality interventions. In A. Thomas & J. Grimes (Eds.), *Best practices in school psychology V* (pp. 177–193). Bethesda, MD: National Association of School Psychologists. Accessed at http://network321.pbworks.com/f/Linking+assessment+to+intervention.pdf on July 1, 2022.

Buffum, A., Mattos, M., & Malone, J. (2018). *Taking action: A handbook for RTI at Work.* Bloomington, IN: Solution Tree Press.

Buffum, A., Mattos, M., & Weber, C. (2009). *Pyramid response to intervention: RTI, professional learning communities, and how to respond when kids don't learn.* Bloomington, IN: Solution Tree Press.

Buffum, A., Mattos, M., & Weber, C. (2010). The why behind RTI. *Educational Leadership, 68*(2), 10–16.

Buffum, A., Mattos, M., & Weber, C. (2012). *Simplifying response to intervention: Four essential guiding principles.* Bloomington, IN: Solution Tree Press.

Conzemius, A. E., & O'Neill, J. (2014). *The handbook for SMART school teams: Revitalizing best practices for collaboration* (2nd ed.). Bloomington, IN: Solution Tree Press.

DuFour, R., DuFour, R., Eaker, R., Many, T. W., & Mattos, M. (2016). *Learning by doing: A handbook for Professional Learning Communities at Work* (3rd ed.). Bloomington, IN: Solution Tree Press.

DuFour, R., DuFour, R., Eaker, R. Mattos, M., & Muhammad, A. (2021). *Revisiting Professional Learning Communities at Work: Proven insights for sustained, substantive school improvement* (2nd ed.). Bloomington, IN: Solution Tree Press.

Garmston, R. J., & Wellman, B. M. (2016). *The adaptive school: A sourcebook for developing collaborative groups* (3rd ed.). Lanham, MD: Rowman & Littlefield.

Hattie, J. (2012). *Visible learning for teachers: Maximizing impact on learning.* New York: Routledge.

National Center for Education Statistics. (2019). *Digest of education statistics.* Accessed at https://nces.ed.gov/programs/digest/d20/tables/dt20_219.90.asp on October 17, 2021.

Stuart, T. S., Heckmann, S., Mattos, M., & Buffum, A. (2018). *Personalized learning in a PLC at Work: Student agency through the four critical questions.* Bloomington, IN: Solution Tree Press.

 **Laura Jo Evans** is associate principal at the International School of Prague, where she is leading the development of learning environments, innovative personalized practices, and professional learning communities (PLCs) in international schools. Previously, she was the early years coordinator at the International Community School (ICS) of Addis Ababa in Ethiopia, a PLC exemplar and an International Baccalaureate Organization (IBO) World School. Laura Jo assisted in developing a strong early childhood program within the Primary Years Programme (PYP) framework; educators participate in teacher research that promotes the rights of students to learn and grow through playful inquiry. Previously an early years educator and collaborative team leader at Singapore American School, Laura Jo participated in extensive professional research and development, traveling to and learning from schools all over the world. This research led to transformational change utilizing effective PLC process collaboration in her early years community and codesigning innovative learning environments and pedagogical transformation with a powerful team of educators. As a lifelong learner, Laura Jo actively continues her work, inspiring play-driven learning as it applies to transient, international learners of all ages. Strengths-based leadership and positive school culture have been a part of her teaching and PLC experience throughout her career. She sees these strengths connected to her responsibility in bringing about positive transformation to organizations where there is growth and cultivation of human potential for students, educators, and leaders alike; this is her joy, passion, and greatest challenge.

Laura Jo is a member of the North American Reggio Emilia Alliance. She remains involved in change leadership in international schools and often presents to parents and key members of international learning communities on play, collaboration, and the power of learning environments. She is working within the International School of Prague toward becoming a IB PYP authorized school.

Laura Jo received a bachelor's degree in elementary education from Calvin University, a master's in international education from Endicott College, and the Principals' Training Center (https://theptc.org) Certificate of International School Leadership.

To book Laura Jo Evans for professional development, contact pd@Solution Tree.com.

CHAPTER 5

Early Years Education and a Pedagogy of *With*

Laura Jo Evans

What is the difference between preschool and early childhood education? Elementary schools have added preschools and prekindergarten classrooms with the mandate that children need to begin the learning journey earlier. If they just learn to read earlier, they will be smarter. Giving students access to an elementary curriculum at a younger age (ages two to five years) to equip them for success later in school is how to accomplish this. While it might be true that having these opportunities and access for young children will boost their learning levels, what does it do to *childhood*? Unfortunately, when early childhood becomes preschool, educators often rob children of their fundamental need to play and research the world around them. *Early childhood* is an opportunity itself. When young children and conscientious educators come together, they create some of the most powerful learning environments and experiences. It is in the sweet spot of early childhood that powerful mathematicians, scientists, artists, writers, actors, and change makers emerge. As philosopher, psychologist, and education reformer John Dewey (1897) stated, "I believe that education, therefore, is a process of living and not a preparation for future living" (p. 78).

The Case for Early Childhood

An eight-month-old child balances on her stomach while placed on the carpet at home. She finds her hands, pushes herself up, and suddenly, her knees bend. She begins to rock back and forth on two knees, and two straight arms. Once tired, she collapses on her stomach and cries out, ready for a break. A few days later, back on hands and knees, one knee and the opposite arm lurch forward. Imbalanced and heavily concentrated, the opposite knee and arm follow. The child has learned to crawl. As an educator, you reflect: "Was the child taught to crawl? Was the child alone? What were the conditions that allowed the child to be successful? What is the role of the parent or caregiver in this situation? If this is learning success, an innate power to achieve, how might it continue throughout life? Do educators and promoters of a peaceful world *not* want the human experience to encompass this power?" And finally, "What are the hurdles in our current world and educational systems that get in the way of such efficacy?"

What if you could find the answer to all these questions in a community of learners? How does this community offer the conditions for all learners to learn with all the capabilities and potentialities they possess? What is the role of the educator in the community of learners? How does the community allow for the continuation of a child's innate power to organize his or her own learning? And sadly, how can a community of learners and its systems, spaces, and structures redirect or even rob children of such efficacy? Is it possible to say to a child, "It's not time to learn to crawl; we are learning something else right now?"

While this innate nurturing is easy to witness in a growing infant-toddler, is it possible for older children? Sugata Mitra, a researcher and theoretical scientist, determined through a series of experiments in slums and rural parts of India that children's innate sense of self and motivation propel them to be naturally self-organized learners (as cited in Toddle, 2020). Mitra conducted several experiments that suggest children can organize themselves in a mainly unsupervised manner to learn about whatever big questions they may have (as cited in Toddle, 2020). With curiosity and the support of the internet (which now transmits any knowledge one might search for), children can learn anything. As daunting as this may seem, and with the array of information and misinformation on the internet, it is paramount that educators join with strong, rich-in-potential self-organized learners on their learning journey to work toward a preferred future. But how?

Mitra gifts readers with the metaphor of the "granny cloud" (as cited in Toddle, 2020). In life, a mother might say to her child, "Come, follow me. I will show you how to do things"—a somewhat daunting responsibility often innate to a mother's role. Mitra, remembering his experience with a grandmother, offers another perspective: granny's. You may hear granny say, "Wow, what's that you have there?" Or, while out exploring, the child may see something interesting, begin to run ahead, and then look back in apprehension of being scolded or scared. Granny, who is with the child, recognizes the wonder of discovery and the desire to explore and says, "You go there. I don't know what's there. I'll go with you" (as cited in Toddle, 2020). The child senses the safety, knows the way, and knows he is not alone. The granny admits, *she doesn't know what's there*, yet they go there together.

What if you consider *learning* to be this trusting, guiding, granny-type relationship and partnership? Is it possible, given the educational systems already in place? It's time to consider your beliefs about learning through a new pedagogy of *with*.

To consider such a pedagogy, you must consider a change in the systematic ways of the past. Then, schools were like factories, producing specific prototypes of citizens, where teachers were the only keepers of knowledge and saw students as empty vessels, some "smart," some not, and controllable. With global values such as equality, inclusion, democracy, empathy, and the rights of children, educators begin again to build a more equitable future. In education, it begins with the youngest learners.

How, then, might early years programs become catalysts for transformational change in all areas of education worldwide? Schools overlook or deprioritize the early years when they enact transformational change, yet the early years provide the essential basis for students as they enter elementary school.

Starting with developing a shared pedagogical understanding, and then moving on to organization and environment design, this chapter focuses on the process of change within an early years program, and looks at how a highly effective, learning-progressive early years program utilizes the professional learning community (PLC) process (Stuart, Heckmann, Buffum, & Mattos, 2018). Using the transdisciplinary, concept-driven International Baccalaureate Primary Years Programme (IB PYP) as an anchor, the daily collective efficacy that occurs will establish a successful way of thinking and learning for students on their learning journey from the very beginning, continuing throughout life.

A Pedagogy of *With*

The metaphor of the grandmother who says, "You go there. I don't know what's there. I'll go with you" is the vision for a pedagogy of *with*. To develop an effective pedagogy of *with* in the early years and beyond, schools must re-examine their beliefs—how they view students, what they are capable of discovering, and how they best learn. Schools must develop shared understandings, implement systems and strategies to support these understandings, and develop co-constructed practices that foster learning.

Shared Understandings

Belief is everything. Recall the example of a child crawling, and you see that a caretaker's belief in a child's natural ability to learn to crawl is a part of the child's success. If that were not the case, the conditions would have been different. In the same way, educators who set out to offer authentic learning experiences for young children must share values for education, beliefs, and understandings of children, their capabilities, and how they learn. According to psychologist and former David Starr Jordan professor of psychology at Stanford University, Albert Bandura's (1994, 1997, 2001) social cognitive theory, educators must develop a collective efficacy. The realization that *all learners learn better together* supports the PLC big idea that all learners can learn at high levels.

People do not live their lives in isolation; many of the things they seek are achievable only through socially interdependent effort. Hence, they must work in coordination with others to secure what they cannot accomplish on their own. Social cognitive theory extends the conception of human agency to *collective agency*:

> People's shared belief in their collective power to produce desired results is a key ingredient of collective agency. Group attainments are the product not only of the shared intentions, knowledge, and skills of its members, but also of the interactive, coordinated, and synergistic dynamics of their transactions. (Bandura, 2001, pp. 13–14)

These shared understandings must align with the school or system as a whole to find the best foot forward. Before teams ask and answer the four PLC critical questions (DuFour, DuFour, Eaker, Many, & Mattos, 2016), educators must collectively ask and collectively agree on the answers to the questions: Who is the child? What is the purpose of school? What is learning? (van Dam, 2019).

Early years educator, leader, and consultant Anne van Dam of the Learning Square (see https://thelearningsquare.nl) challenged teams of early years teachers at the International Community School (ICS) of Addis Ababa, Ethiopia, to ask these questions. A pedagogical coordinator led the early years team composed of four groups of children aged two to six years and approximately twenty teachers and educational assistants. The team participated in action research that led members to examine and develop a set of collective beliefs that drives the team's approach to learning in the early years. These beliefs, which align with the school's foundational principles, drive all daily curricular decisions and practices. Figure 5.1 shows the team-developed powerful set of beliefs.

The Early Years at the International Community School of Addis Ababa: Who We Are

Be, Connect, Grow, Transform: Myself, My Community, My World

Being: Our Image of the Child

We value each individual child as unique, strong, capable, creative, and full of wonder. As researchers and bearers of rights, children are socially connected and actively participate in their learning process. We believe that as active participants, children have the right to express themselves and make meaning of their world in many ways and at their own pace.

Children research their world, while educators research learning.

We view educators not as transmitters of knowledge, but rather curators of learning experiences. Educators and children are both researchers in the learning process.

Our learning spaces, indoors and out, are inviting and promote curiosity. We purposefully plan, often with children, in response to our beliefs about capable children, creating rich conditions in which children learn.

Connecting: The Learning Process

We believe play, being social and symbolic, is the driving force for learning. *Play* is a social process, and children construct meaning during interactions with others, including capable and competent educators. Through play, children at ICS participate in meaningful investigations and inquiries, using the PYP framework and the concept-based and inquiry-driven ICS learning process as anchors, with children at the center of the learning process.

Growing: Symbolic Exploration and Expression

We believe symbolic play and expression are the starting points for a strong learning community. We support children in their expression and in using all their senses to make meaning through many symbolic processes, including movement, painting, transformation, mathematics, drawing, mark making, socio-dramatics, building, sculpture, and sound, singing, and rhythm. These areas of expression help build a strong cognitive, social, and communicative foundation for future learning in the elementary years and beyond.

Transforming: Our Local and Global Community

We believe children are actively involved in reshaping the community (Rinaldi, 2021), and, therefore, their world.

Our learning community is full of hope, and its unique children reshape it.

Source: © 2019 by the International Community School of Addis Ababa. Adapted with permission; Rinaldi, 2021.

FIGURE 5.1: Collective beliefs driving the learning in the early years.

Systems and Strategies

Coauthors Richard DuFour, Rebecca DuFour, Robert Eaker, Thomas W. Many, and Mike Mattos (2016) define a *professional learning community* as "an ongoing process in which educators work collaboratively in recurring cycles of collective inquiry and action research in order to achieve better results *for* the students they serve" (p. 10; emphasis added). According to this definition, all curricular decisions and ultimate control over learning are in the hands of the school and educators. However, in the current global landscape, where many bring equity and fundamental rights into question worldwide, it is important to consider where power and control lie.

PLC experts Timothy Stuart, Sascha Heckmann, Mike Mattos, and Austin Buffum (2018) discuss the importance of future-ready learning. The future is here. Therefore, what does it mean to be *future ready*? Is this now the purpose of learning? Is this now why learning must shift toward being highly effective and learning progressive? While there is no doubt a constantly shifting global economy and connectivity with the rest of the world impact the need for educational reform, educators must not abandon the innate human desire for connection and relationships. Relationships are everywhere—living, nonliving, and once living. Educators must include the *why* because the world is changing, they must adapt along with it, and they must still hold fast to the true north of human relationships and the responsibility that comes with living in relationships (Malaguzzi, 1993). Therefore, as Mitra's (as cited in Toddle, 2020) research states, Do educators really need to join learners in a new way? Or might it be the case that this has always *been* the way, and education reform in certain countries got off track? Education reformers Lev Vygotsky (1978), Paulo Freire (1968/2018), and John Dewey (1938), to name a few, argued this for decades. And now, thanks to globalization and connection, educators can learn from and with educators in other countries about how they go about learning. Might the international learning community have an opportunity to model equity and unity by adopting a pedagogy that unites nations? In doing this, might PLCs take on a new effort to "achieve better results" (DuFour et al., 2016, p. 10) *with* the students they serve, as opposed to *for*?

Stuart and colleagues (2018) shift the paradigm. They remind educators that for students to be future ready, they must equip students with more than what they simply teach them. Stuart and colleagues (2018) point to education professor and director of the Melbourne Education Research Institute in Australia John Hattie's (2009) findings that impactful student learning takes place when the conditions involve students self-monitoring and self-assessing their own learning. Stuart and colleagues (2018) ascertain that schools must be both highly effective (with a guaranteed and viable curriculum) and learning progressive (the approach to learning that includes deepening content and cultivating important 21st century skills and dispositions) to best equip students for an unforeseen future. Highly effective schools incorporate the PLC process to maintain their effectiveness and alignment, while also being learning progressive in their pedagogical approach through nurturing student agency that motivates all learners to learn at high levels. Stuart and colleagues (2018) suggest using the strategy of the four PLC critical questions from the standpoint of the student asking and answering them to grasp this shift in thinking.

1. What do *I* want to know, understand, and be able to do?
2. How will *I* demonstrate that I have learned it?
3. What will *I* do when I am not learning?
4. What will *I* do when I have already learned it?

Personalized Learning in a PLC at Work provides a comprehensive road map to the personalization of learning, offering well-researched strategies toward becoming a highly effective and learning-progressive school where all learners feel empowered, equipped, nurtured, and respected as agents in the learning process (Stuart et al., 2018).

Co-Construction of Learning

Schools should ask the following set of questions for a school context that demonstrates the relationship between being highly effective and learning progressive as an anchor for fostering a strong and sustainable co-constructed pedagogy of *with* (DuFour et al., 2016).

1. What do *we* want to know, understand, and be able to do?
2. How will *we* demonstrate that we have learned it?
3. What will *we* do when we are not learning?
4. What will *we* do when we have already learned it?

The Reggio Emilia Approach inspired the ICS early years pedagogy statement that says, "Children research their world, while educators research learning" (Reggio Children, 2020; as cited in Rinaldi, 2021; see figure 5.1, page 105). Educators of all age groups, collaborating with one another and their students in a community of learners, deepen this practice. As Stuart and colleagues (2018) demonstrate in *Personalized Learning in a PLC at Work*, this is not only for young learners but *all* learners. All learners have agency—they are born with initiative and curiosity. Committing to a pedagogy of *with* schoolwide requires all stakeholders to commit to a life of learning. The PLC process and the IB PYP framework set up educators and students equitably to do just that.

Highly Effective and Learning-Progressive Early Years Practice

Stuart and colleagues' (2018) definition of a highly effective and learning-progressive school perfectly describes how young children learn:

> Schools that are both highly effective and learning progressive . . . have highly focused disciplinary outcomes, a clearly articulated trans-disciplinary skills curriculum, and a learning progressive pedagogical approach that emphasizes specific lifelong learning outcomes. (p. 15)

Curious at their core, children make meaning of the world around them as young researchers. Exploring their world with all their senses, they engage with phenomena across all disciplines naturally. For example, children will play with sand and water, making canals and tunnels, testing theories of trajectory and motion as water flows and then overflows into a pool. They change the flow of water by digging deeper canals, adding sand to obstruct the flow like an engineer, and testing the function of a system. They converse and negotiate with their peers, perhaps arguing or non-verbally supporting by offering a new piece of equipment to try. Others nearby make up stories as they sail an imaginary boat down their created river. Here, the children engage in scientific concepts, mathematical thinking, and social negotiation, and build symbolic literacy skills as well as fine-motor skills, among other learning. In this natural learning process called *play*, children have power over their research choices and accomplishments; they are agents and protagonists in the learning. To support a highly effective and learning-progressive system in which students have ample opportunity for play and agency, there are several key practices the IB PYP supports through the following four central features:

1. Play

2. Relationships

3. Learning spaces

4. Symbolic play and exploration (International Baccalaureate Organization [IBO], 2018a)

These practices are also interwoven throughout the four critical questions of a PLC (see table 5.1).

TABLE 5.1: A Highly Effective Learning-Progressive Early Years Practice: Co-Construction of the Learning Process

PLC Focus	Example
A guaranteed and viable curriculum that includes disciplinary knowledge: the agreed-on knowledge, skills, and understandings that serve a student's learning, growth, and development PLC critical question one: What do we need to know, understand, and be able to do?	Identifiable individual developmental milestones (for example, GOLD Objectives for Development and Learning [Teaching Strategies, 2010] continuum, yardsticks, ages, and stages) PYP program of inquiry (see chapter 1, page 13) PYP Q1 document (see figure 2.2, page 28) Disciplinary learning standards
Culture of collective efficacy: The belief that learning does not happen in isolation; educators are more effective in causing learning for *all* learners (Bandura, 2001) PLC critical question two: How will we know we're getting there? What are students communicating or researching? Where are they telling us they want to go next (both verbally and nonverbally) through play?	Educators collaborate about documented observational data, assist one another in the interpretation of the student's learning process, and offer ideas, contexts, and materials to relaunch according to the direction the student is communicating he or she is ready to move in.
Evidence-based reflection: The process of how educators document observations to bring to the collaborative team meeting: a pedagogy of listening (Rinaldi, 2021) PLC critical question two: How will we get there? What are we observing and listening for? What theories emerge through a learning experience, through play?	Teams determine *what* they are observing on a particular day and record observations on an app, a common template, or grid to bring to the collaborative team meeting for interpretation. (See figure 5.2, page 110 for an example.)
Learner responsive with flexible instruction: A belief that learning is not linear; rather, systems are appropriately in place, such as learning spaces, materials, educator expertise and roles, and documentation processes to design conditions and experiences in response to learner curiosity and challenge. Student and adult learners participate in the inquiry learning process as a group and in real time. PLC critical questions three and four: What do we (both teacher and student) do when we're curious about something new? What is the student's zone of proximal development (Vygotsky, 1978)? How do we respond or take action when things are too hard (critical question three) or too easy (critical question four)?	Group response: Once they interpret data or evidence, teams determine what skills to embed into the relaunched learning experiences for groups and individuals, as well as what new teacher and student research to document. Educators compare lists of students they have not yet observed and agree to gather evidence for these learners. Individual responses in real time: Learners and educators play or investigate together with open-ended materials, such as clay, blocks, fabric, paint, paper, glue, sand, water, collected "treasures," and so on. As students engage with materials during play or a proposed learning experience, they are sometimes personally challenged, or curious, to create or design with the materials, either to a specific interest-based end or toward a discovered product. When the experience becomes too hard or too easy, a peer helps the individual students redirect themselves, or a skilled educator offers a strategy or material to assist.

Source: Adapted from Stuart et al., 2018.

Week of: Educator:	Context, Intentions, or Research Question:	
What? Narrative notes that relate to the context or intention	**So What?** What is the significance of this observation? What interests and concepts are arising?	**Now What?** Possible ways for students to explore their thinking in more complex ways

Source: © 2021 by the International School of Addis Ababa. Adapted with permission.

FIGURE 5.2: ICS early years observation template.

*Visit **go.SolutionTree.com/PLCbooks** for a free reproducible version of this figure.*

What Do We Want to Know, Understand, and Be Able to Do?

In a highly effective and learning-progressive early years program, the curricular focus becomes the transdisciplinary skills and development of the learner identity. Still, discipline-specific outcomes remain clear and known to the educator. (See the description of the IB PYP critical question one document in chapter 2, page 21, where educators embed knowledge, skills, and dispositions in the transdisciplinary unit of inquiry, as well as strongly connect them to disciplinary outcomes.) The IB PYP outlines the disciplinary scope and sequence (IBO, n.d.), and can also support specific skills connected to a certain set of well-researched learning standards or objectives (such as the Common Core or GOLD Objectives for Development and Learning [as cited in Teaching Strategies, 2010]), or a specific country's required learning outcomes. These standards are all in service of the conceptual learning you are aiming for.

How Will We Know We Are Learning?

As the educational landscape shifts from a focus on teaching to a focus on learning, it is critical to approach learning from the learner's perspective. While many who are implementing the PLC process's four critical questions begin with question one (What do we want students to know and be able to do?), in early years education using a personalized learning approach, educators should begin with question two (How do we know if they have learned it?). What is the student showing us he or she is curious about? What is the student communicating through research and wonder? Therefore, although educators know their curriculum (the answers to critical question one), students each drive the curriculum as opposed to the curriculum driving students. As the learner actively participates in the process of learning through both child-initiated play or adult-initiated playful experiences, the educators observe this process; interpret concepts, interests, and thinking processes that arise from the experience; and relaunch or enhance the experience, if necessary, for deeper learning. Because educators know the curriculum well, they know what learning is taking place during the engagement and can document the experience as evidence of learning. Educators also know they need to challenge a student who is *not* engaged, either through conversation, new materials, redirecting play, or using various other strategies. This process of identifying an experience as "not too easy, not too hard" is known as the *zone of proximal development* (Vygotsky, 1978). Teachers and early years educators together best carry out the process of documentation and intentional cultivation of learning experiences. The teachers document the process, making it visible to the students, families, and the learning community. (See figure 5.3 for an example of documented learning.) This is the *co-construction of learning* (Stuart et al., 2018). Consider the following examples from practice.

The Concept of Connection and Feelings	
While noticing the documentation on the wall, Bryn said to Stella, "Thanks for getting me ice." He then noticed a small scrape on Stella's forehead and told Ms. Sisay she should get her ice too. Bryn is thankful for Stella's act of kindness. He shows us that he has trust in his environment and the people in it to care for him. We see his growing sense of empathy and conceptual understanding of connection as he expresses a desire to help Stella with her scrape—making connections across contexts.	

Source: © 2021 by Laura Kent-Davidson. Used with permission.

FIGURE 5.3: Learning story documentation example.

A group of learners is engaging with clay. They become frustrated that the clay (with which they wish to make a "cake") is not molding appropriately and begin to walk away. An educator or another peer observes, identifies the challenge, and suggests a way to make the clay more malleable or offers a different material to make it stronger. Together, they solve the challenge and both the educator (or peer) and students participate in a joyful and successful reciprocal exchange. The educator takes a photo and makes a note of the process for how the students assist one another, with the goal of observing evidence of students problem solving together.

An individual learner brings a tray of sand to a tricycle and tries to balance the tray on the tricycle, desiring to transport the tray. The tray begins to topple, and the student tests different ways to balance the tray. The tray still topples. The student quickly catches it and brings a wagon over to see if the tray will fit better in the wagon. An educator offers a small rope to the student, who ties the wagon to the tricycle, places the sand tray into the wagon, and adds two more buckets of sand to the wagon, ready to transport the materials successfully. Prior to the experience, the educator decided to observe the learning environment for evidence of students participating in the learning process through play. (See figure 5.4.) The educator records the experience, takes this to his collaborative team, and together members note the process of inquiry (addressing question one), action (addressing question two), and reflection (addressing question three) the student participated in within the short span of three minutes. The team then composes a learning story (see figure 5.3, page 111) to communicate to families and records it as evidence of the individual student's learning journey in a digital portfolio.

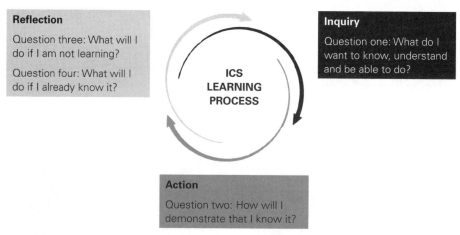

Source: © 2018 by the International Community School of Addis Ababa. Adapted with permission.

FIGURE 5.4: The ICS learning process.

A student wants to enter imaginative play with dolls with another group of students but does not yet have the verbal language to communicate her desire. There are no dolls left. She finds a small ball and wraps it in a blanket and shows her peers that her materials symbolize a doll. They move aside and make space for her to enter the learning story. An educator, with the goal of observing students' intentional interactions, records this learning story and brings it to the team as evidence of social engagement. The team decides to offer more materials in the environment for students to create more items for imaginative play. Members also compose a learning story of the group's experience and process as evidence of social growth and development, as well as symbolic play and exploration, and communicate this to families on a digital communication portfolio.

These examples involve the central features of the early years learning the IB PYP describes: a learning *environment* that fosters inquiry, investigation, and unstructured time for *play* (IBO, n.d.). Powerful *relationships* are present both with caring, collaborative, conscientious educators, as well as relationships with materials, the environment, and peers. Students engage in *symbolic exploration and expression*, building themselves important preliteracy and prenumeracy foundational conceptual understandings.

Central Features of the PYP in the Early Years

The PYP highlights the IB learner profile as being a key component of the development of the competent, curious learner (IBO, n.d.). The *IB learner profile* is a list of attributes the school values and can assist individuals in becoming "responsible members of local, national and global communities" (IBO, 2018a). The PYP believes in the power of the agentic learner. The IBO (2018a) regards *agency* as being about students taking initiative and directing their own learning in powerful ways and with others, as Bandura (1994) writes. *Agency*, therefore, builds a sense of community where learners understand each other's needs and contributions (IBO, 2018a). The PYP publication *The Learner* offers four central features of early years learning: (1) play, (2) relationships, (3) learning spaces, and (4) symbolic exploration and expression (IBO, 2018a). Educators co-construct units of inquiry with these central features in mind, paying careful attention to student interests and relationships as entry points for deeper conceptual understandings.

The previous examples allow for the highest expression of learner agency, as educators take on the role of the facilitator, listener, observer, documenter, co-interpreter, collaborator, and co-participant in the student's learning process, among many other roles. Teachers give up control over *how* the student participates and foster a strong image of the curious student as competent and capable of being an active participant in the co-construction of learning. Just as a child, with the right environmental conditions and supportive educator or caregiver presence, can learn to crawl, a student can learn a hundred times over all the answers to the big questions yet to be discovered to make the world a more peaceful, equitable place of existence. Finally, the educators and students participate in the process of authentic learning and discovery. Using the highly effective learning-progressive components of the PYP and collective efficacy of a collaborative PLC, educators and students can participate in a powerful pedagogy of *with*. Table 5.2 outlines the central features of learning in the early years (IBO, 2018a).

TABLE 5.2: What Does Learning Look Like in the PYP Early Years?

Move Away From	Move Toward
Predetermined time structures and routines	Flexible timeframes and routines responsive to students' needs
Pedagogy that centers on instructional processes for students and is teacher led	Play co-constructed between students and teachers
Repeated large-group experiences as the basis for all learning	Whole-group experiences at pertinent learning moments
Literacy and numeracy experiences that develop skill sets through memorization and worksheets	Literacy and numeracy experiences that develop a wide range of playful, inquiry-based explorations into symbolic and representational learning
Development of self-regulation supported through praise and punishment	Development of self-regulation through play, modeling behaviors, language, group games, and music and movement
Units of inquiry comprising predetermined learning engagements on concepts that are precursors to later learning	Units of inquiry that are iterative and flexible, centering on concepts of significance in the lives of students
Learning spaces that promote dependence on others (that is, where teachers store, control, and access materials for students)	Learning spaces that promote high levels of independence, offering students opportunities to access materials and manage learning
Learning spaces where the teachers timetable play at specific times for specific purposes	Learning spaces where play and choice are central features of everyday learning
Learning spaces where teachers restrict and timetable learning experiences	Flexible learning spaces that provide for many different learning experiences at all times
Learning spaces where teachers ask students to engage with particular learning tasks at particular times	Learning spaces where students have sustained time to select their learning experiences based on their interests and social connections
Assessment that measures predetermined sets of skills against developmental norms for grouping and ranking purposes	Assessment that monitors and documents students' learning against individual developmental milestones and celebrates achievements at times pertinent to individuals
Measuring learning solely by tracking the progress of the group against learning goals	Responding to the individual learning and development journey as well as valuing and recording the learning of the whole group

Conclusion

This chapter emphasized the importance of authentic early childhood learning. The key to implementing a sustainable, highly effective, and learning-progressive early learning project in a school is by first aligning philosophically to a constructivist, collaborative approach to early childhood. The commitment to guaranteeing the rights of childhood by meeting students in their natural sense of curiosity through a pedagogy of *with* is of utmost importance. Furthermore, the successful implementation of the PYP specific to the early years includes important components such as play, symbolic exploration and expression, engaging learning spaces, and authentic relationships. Strongly committed, cohesive, collaborative, teacher-researcher teams anchor the guarantee that all student-citizens, full of wonder at the core, learn powerfully at the highest level.

 # Next Steps

Consider the following suggested actions for getting started on becoming highly effective and then moving to the next level by becoming learning progressive.

Getting Started on Being Highly Effective

- Form collaborative teams that meet regularly to participate in collective inquiry about early years pedagogy and learning practices.

- Research and develop shared beliefs and understandings with early years educators and leaders around the questions, Who is the child? What is the purpose of school? and What is learning? Collaboration with outside consultants, experts in the community, or both can help answer these questions. This process could include visiting other schools or programs, participating in professional learning opportunities, and doing action research. Suggestions for research include, but are not limited to, the Reggio Emilia Approach; Reggio Emilia Approach–inspired PYP schools; and programs where student-initiated play and adult-initiated learning experiences, as well as co-constructed learning, are core values.

- Examine your current practices and programs. Determine how they align with your shared beliefs and values, and determine what can be done to adapt these practices and programs so they can contribute to (and not hinder) what your school desires.

- Ensure teachers and leaders are aligned and equipped with the desired practices and goals, including understanding about the role of the teacher, student, and learning environment in the inquiry process.

- Ensure a guaranteed and viable curriculum is in place.

Moving to the Next Level—Becoming Learning Progressive

- Ensure the guaranteed and viable curriculum is concept driven and transdisciplinary, with students at the center of the learning process.

- Design systems for documenting, monitoring, measuring, and reporting on knowledge, skills, and transdisciplinary learning outcomes. This includes becoming familiar with learning stories, digital communication platforms, and evidence-gathering tools to ensure all students are learning at their own pace in effective ways.

- Co-construct flexibly timed units of inquiry or student-initiated projects that project transdisciplinary learning experiences and incorporate essential disciplinary and social-emotional learning outcomes.

- Ensure the environment is innovative, inviting, and a key facilitator in the learning process of students.

 # References and Resources

Bandura, A. (1994). *Self-efficacy*. In R. J. Corsini (Ed.), *Encyclopedia of psychology* (2nd ed., Vol. 3, pp. 368–369). New York: Wiley.

Bandura, A. (1997). *Self-efficacy: The exercise of control*. New York: Freeman.

Bandura, A. (2001). Social cognitive theory: An agentic perspective. *Annual Review of Psychology, 52*(1), 1–26.

Cadwell, L. B. (1997). *Bringing Reggio Emilia home: An innovative approach to early childhood education*. New York: Teachers College Press.

Carr, M., & Lee, W. (2019). *Learning stories in practice*. Thousand Oaks, CA: SAGE.

Dewey, J. (1897). My pedagogic creed. *School Journal, 54*, 77–80. Accessed at http://dewey.pragmatism.org/creed.htm on July 6, 2022.

Dewey, J. (1938). *Experience and education*. New York: Macmillan.

DuFour, R., DuFour, R., Eaker, R., Many, T. W., & Mattos, M. (2016). *Learning by doing: A handbook for Professional Learning Communities at Work* (3rd ed.). Bloomington, IN: Solution Tree Press.

Freire, P. (2018). *Pedagogy of the oppressed* (50th anniversary ed.; M. B. Ramos, Trans.). New York: Bloomsbury. (Original work published 1968)

Hattie, J. (2009). *Visible learning: A synthesis of over 800 meta-analyses relating to achievement*. London: Routledge.

International Baccalaureate Organization. (n.d.). *Primary Years Programme*. Accessed at www.ibo.org/programmes/primary-years-programme on April 15, 2022.

International Baccalaureate Organization. (2018a). *The learner*. Accessed at https://resources.ibo.org/data/the-learner_fc17a71a-2344-4b26-84cb-caca3a02750d/the-learner-en_d32875a1-8611-4de3-9f7d-14a22127adc2.pdf on May 20, 2022.

International Baccalaureate Organization. (2018b). *Mathematics scope and sequence*. Accessed at www.ibo.org on May 20, 2022.

Malaguzzi, L. (1993). For an education based on relationships. *Young Children*, *49*(1), 9–12.

Reggio Children. (2020). *Reggio Emilia Approach*. Accessed at www.reggiochildren.it/en/reggio-emilia-approach on February 28, 2022.

Rinaldi, C. (2021). *In dialogue with Reggio Emilia: Listening, researching and learning* (2nd ed.). New York: Routledge, Taylor & Francis.

Stuart, T. S. (Ed.). (2016). *Global perspectives: Professional Learning Communities at Work in international schools*. Bloomington, IN: Solution Tree Press.

Stuart, T. S., Heckmann, S., Mattos, M., & Buffum, A. (2018). *Personalized learning in a PLC at Work: Student agency through the four critical questions*. Bloomington, IN: Solution Tree Press.

Teaching Strategies. (2010). *Objectives for development & learning*. Accessed at https://troy.edu/_assets/dothan-campus/_documents/goldprogressionsen.pdf on July 8, 2022.

Toddle. (2020, May). *Children and the internet—New ways for new times* [Video file.] Accessed at https://vimeo.com/419298150 on February 28, 2022.

van Dam, A. (2019). *Constant conversations: Unpacking pedagogy—Change and the pervasiveness of "developmentally appropriate practice."* Accessed at https://unpackingourpedagogy.blogspot.com/2019/04/change-and -pervasiveness-of.html on February 28, 2022.

Vygotsky, L. S. (1978). *Mind in society: The development of higher psychological processes.* Cambridge, MA: Harvard University Press.

Eyerusalem Kifle is a second-grade teacher at the International Community School (ICS) of Addis Ababa in Ethiopia. She served as the educational assistant coordinator and as part of the elementary leadership team, and co-constructed professional development modules and provided learning opportunities for educational assistants.

Eyerusalem has been an educator since 2005, with a background as a teaching assistant, teacher, grade-level team leader, and curriculum coordinator in a variety of school settings in Addis Ababa. Her educational experiences range from working in a predominantly low-income minority school to some of the most affluent and high-performing schools in Ethiopia. She's also taught middle school Ethiopian studies using a personalized learning approach. Eyerusalem's strong belief in developing schools responsive to students' needs and establishing a culture of high expectations has resulted in marked improvement in various schools. She has presented on personalized learning in Ethiopian studies in Addis Ababa.

Eyerusalem received a bachelor's degree in English language and literature from Addis Ababa University, a master's degree in education from the State University of New York, and a teaching certification from Moreland University.

To learn more about Eyerusalem's work, follow @EbonyKifle on Twitter.

To book Eyerusalem Kifle for professional development, contact pd@Solution Tree.com.

CHAPTER 6

The Educational Assistant in the PYP and PLC

Eyerusalem Kifle

Educators in the 21st century consistently ask and strive to answer the question, "What are we preparing our students for?" The conventional education system that prevailed in the manufacturing era is no longer the best learning environment to ensure every student learns at a higher level. Modern-day educators feel responsible to prepare students for an unpredictable future in a new digitally advanced world and are not even sure if the jobs of today will exist when students enter the professional world.

If a school wants to ensure every student learns at the highest level and is prepared for the unknown future ahead, then teachers cannot be left to achieve this goal single-handedly and without active cooperation with other educators. Researcher John Hattie (2012) emphasizes in his work on collective teacher efficacy that when teachers share responsibilities, provide feedback, and work collaboratively, they are more likely to have a positive impact on one another's and students' learning.

Since the beginning of universal compulsory education, it has been common for teachers to work independently. In a traditional classroom structure, educational assistants provide help for teachers and support for learners, and many policymakers still hold this view. However, this traditional structure seems to be changing as educational assistants are doing what previously was unthinkable—*teaching students*—as the definition of learning evolves over time. For example, the Open University's (n.d.) foundation degree for educational assistants makes explicit: this is a degree in primary *teaching and learning*, not a degree in *supporting learning*. Teaching assistants, according to author Celia Dillow (2010), are involved in jobs that "look like teaching" as well as more traditional supporting responsibilities (p. 8). According to coauthors Peter Blatchford, Anthony Russell, and Rob Webster (2012), if teaching assistants have a "direct pedagogical, instructional relationship with pupils" they are teaching (p. 140).

Even though most would agree that educational assistants play an essential role in schools around the world, they are often left out in planning for professional development and change. This chapter shares the steps schools should take to include educational assistants in the process of implementing personalized learning and some of the benefits of such an approach. The chapter also provides working examples from a school that has explicitly included educational assistants in professional development for professional learning communities (PLCs), which has led to educational assistants being active participants in instructional planning, playing the role of the *fourth teacher* (the parents, classroom teachers, and the classroom environment being the first three).

Shifting From a Teacher-Centered Approach

One of the biggest reasons for the shift in the role of educational assistants is the evolution from the conventional way of teaching to *student-centered learning*, which recognizes students are not empty vessels for teachers to fill with knowledge; rather, they have prior knowledge and learn best by *learning how to learn* as educators meet students where they are and ensure they succeed. According to the constructivist theories of education that Swiss clinical psychologist Jean Piaget champions, children cognitively construct knowledge and meaning through new experiences and interactions as opposed to rote memorization (as cited in Huitt & Hummel, 2003). This view of education is at odds with the traditional way of teaching, where teachers impart all knowledge without regard to or input from students. This traditional approach does not have room for personalization or collaboration with other educators and hinders educational assistants from actively and directly participating to constructively impact student learning.

This paradigm shift from traditional teaching to active student participation has caused the role of the educational assistant to change gradually in the classroom. Educational assistants, once considered teachers' aides who make photocopies and run errands, are invaluable to the PLC process and the International Baccalaureate Primary Years Programme (IB PYP) framework when used to their full potential.

Maximizing Student Learning in the PLC Process With Educational Assistants

As you've learned in previous chapters, PLC experts Richard DuFour, Rebecca DuFour, Robert Eaker, Thomas W. Many, and Mike Mattos (2016) define PLCs as "an ongoing process in which educators work collaboratively in recurring cycles of collective inquiry and action research to achieve better results for the students they serve" (p. 10). When targeting essential disciplinary outcomes, the collaborative teacher team is responsible for the path and pace of learning. The team must ensure it teaches the guaranteed and viable curriculum (see chapter 2, page 21, for more information) and all students are able to demonstrate mastery of the intended learning outcomes. Teams do this by asking and answering the four critical questions of a PLC (DuFour et al., 2016). As DuFour and colleagues (2016) clearly state, adults working in a school who directly impact student learning should be part of the PLC process. So how crucial is it to revise school policies and take measures to include educational assistants, who play a vital role in ensuring students learn at a higher level? When schools include educational assistants in the PLC process, it paves the way for them to meet regularly with other educators and address the four critical questions as a team:

1. What do we expect students to know, understand, and be able to do?
2. How will we know when they have learned it?
3. How will we respond when they don't learn it?
4. How will we respond when they already know it? (DuFour et al., 2016, p. 34)

Answering these critical questions together allows educational assistants, along with other educators, to plan clear, consistent, and obtainable learning targets; develop common formative assessments that align to these targets; and develop interventions and extensions for students who need additional support or the opportunity to go beyond the articulated curriculum. Therefore, schools should inform educational assistants about student needs, plan the next steps, and enforce best practices to ensure each student learns at a higher level.

When it comes to implementing new policies and change, it is necessary to include educational assistants in the process with deep conversations among leadership teams, teachers, and other educational assistants. Another obstacle for including educational assistants is finding collaboration time in the schedule. The leadership team plays a vital role in allocating time in the schedule to allow educational assistants to play a more significant role in the PLC process.

Providing Professional Learning

To participate fully, schools should involve educational assistants in professional learning about the PLC process (including the four critical questions of a PLC and personalized learning) to ensure all educational assistants actively participate in the PLC and help students learn at a higher level. Collaborative team leaders play an important role in facilitating the opportunities for educational assistants to share their ideas and make them feel safe and that they belong in the group; this does not always come naturally. Encourage educational assistants to identify areas in which they would like to grow (for example, personalized learning, PYP, response to intervention (RTI), behavior management strategies, supporting independence and individual thinking, assessment, documentation, and reading and writing workshops).

Actively Asking the Four Critical Questions in a PLC

Creating learning environments that foster high levels of learning and learning engagement for all students requires bringing all educators, including educational assistants, into collaborative conversations. This section aims to show what it looks like when educational assistants are included in the PLC process and meet regularly with their teacher colleagues to ask and answer the four critical questions. This inclusion enhances the collaborative team by adding to the diversity and perspectives of the team members.

What Do We Expect Students to Know, Understand, and Be Able to Do?

Answering the first critical question establishes clarity about what teams want students to learn and focuses the guaranteed and viable curriculum. As DuFour and colleagues (2016) state, as educators answer question one collaboratively, they are identifying proficiency standards, unwrapping each standard, identifying the learning target for each unit of instruction, and rewording each learning target in student-friendly language. Involving educational assistants in answering the first critical question makes them aware of exactly what teachers expect students to know so the educational assistants can teach small groups.

At the International Community School (ICS) of Addis Ababa in Ethiopia, most educational assistants come from a teaching background and have multiple degrees; therefore, they are important members of the PLC who actively address the four critical questions. Full-time learning coaches and curriculum coordinators assist the educational assistants in each division. As a school, ICS values professional development for educational assistants, and staff provide numerous opportunities for professional development ICS hosts, as well as online courses. Faculty members each receive a professional development budget as part of their contract with ICS. There is a designated education assistant coach to coordinate and provide professional development. Providing ongoing professional development for educational assistants ensures their efficiency for helping students learn at the highest level.

Small-group teaching is probably the best space for students to digest, think through, and integrate ideas they've encountered from other sources (such as lectures or books). It's usually the best way for students to grapple with tricky ideas that, once understood, transform students' perspectives on a subject (Jaques, 1992, 2007). Educational assistants can play a significant role in starting a discussion, giving students plenty of time to think about the implications of new ideas; helping students integrate the discussion with their existing knowledge and understanding; providing prompts when necessary to keep the discussion going or moving it in a new direction; and drawing the session to a close by helping students acknowledge what they've learned and where to go next to keep learning.

How Will We Know When They Have Learned It?

Research shows one of the most powerful learning tools to answer critical question two is a well-crafted common formative assessment that aligns to each learning outcome (Hattie & Yates, 2014). Doing this gives students and the teacher data on student progress toward proficiency of the intended learning target (Hattie & Yates, 2014). Educational assistants can significantly contribute to giving formal and informal assessments, writing observations, and analyzing data collaboratively to inform their teaching and make changes to teaching points.

How Will We Respond When They Don't Learn?

From my years of experience as an educational assistant and teacher, I strongly believe educational assistants have informally played a crucial role in answering critical question three and taking action when some students do not learn. When students struggle to reach the desired level of proficiency, well-trained educational assistants can intervene. Hattie's (2009) meta-analysis finds an effect size greater than one standard deviation when educators effectively implement RTI. This makes RTI one of the most powerful strategies to ensure all students learn at a high level. Schools should train educational assistants in RTI to ensure each student achieves mastery. After looking at assessment data, educational assistants can focus on students who are not making adequate progress in the regular classroom and then provide increasingly intensive instruction matched to student needs on the basis of levels of performance and rates of progress. Educational assistants can provide instruction in small-group settings in addition to instruction in the general curriculum. These interventions might focus on the areas of reading and mathematics. An intervention may require a longer period of time, but it should generally not exceed a grading period. Educational assistants can collect and analyze data to identify students who continue to show too little progress at a level of intervention and suggest more intensive interventions (Tier 3).

How Will We Respond When They Already Know It?

PLC critical question four asks, "How will we extend the learning for students who are already proficient?" (DuFour et al., 2016, p. 36). Schools should challenge this often-neglected group of students to inquire deeper, take action, or become an expert on a topic to solve a real-life problem with the guidance of an educational assistant. For example, the educational assistant's role apart from the teacher's role could be to take the extension group and support students to research and identify areas for possible action research. This might involve the following steps: Students make a list of inquiry questions about a global issue they are interested in. They determine the best solutions for evaluating the research question (such as reading, community interviews, or a survey). They design a comprehensive and innovative advocacy project based on the research. They select sources of information that will assist in answering their inquiry questions (books, websites, interviews, and so on). Students then step into the role of a leader of an advocacy group heading up the distribution of funds to a community. Students design a plan to convince stakeholders of the project's viability. They create an innovative project to support a community in need and gain support from the local community to solve a real-life problem.

Creating the Learning Environment

Educational assistants can play a significant role in creating a learning environment that promotes collaboration and a shared sense of purpose and belonging. An environment respects the agency of "rich and powerful learners" (Edwards, Gandini, & Forman 1998), inspires creativity and innovation, and recognizes experimentation and failure as an integral part of the learning process. The student impacts the environment and, in turn, the environment impacts the student (Bronfenbrenner, 1979). Every action in the environment brings about a reaction, and it is through this reciprocal process that learning occurs. For example, while the ground does not teach a child, the child learns about the breakability of a glass object when he or she drops it on the ground and sees and hears the glass crack. Students also define their identity in learning environments (Edwards et al., 1998). Educational assistants collaboratively create a learning environment that considers pedagogy, safety, social and emotional well-being, and the virtual and physical spaces where learning occurs. For example, educational assistants might create centers for mathematics, reading, writing, and a unit of inquiry. They look at lessons to ensure each center has enough related resources that align with the unit. The educational assistants make sure classroom libraries contain a range of related resources (fiction, nonfiction, fairy tales, poetry, magazines, and persuasive writing). Another example is educational assistants developing unit of inquiry boards with inquiry cycles and teaching materials so students can easily access information and learn from their environment.

Becoming the Fourth Teacher

Educators in PLC schools understand being in a PLC is not participating in a program in which there is a prescribed curriculum or dictated instructional practices on a master schedule. Rather, *functioning as a PLC* is participating in a continuous process focused on and dedicated to a shared mission of ensuring high levels of learning for every student (DuFour et al., 2016). This focus on learning unites and guides the organization's collaborative efforts; the organization asks the question, "Will this action improve student learning?" to assess all its policies, practices, and procedures (DuFour et al., 2016). Because individual educators cannot possibly possess all the knowledge, skills, and resources they need to ensure high levels of learning for every student, members of teams work collaboratively and take collective responsibility for all students' success. This shows the importance of leveraging the use of educational assistants as the fourth teachers who collaboratively plan and share responsibilities to ensure students learn at a higher level, from assisting in identifying what students should know and be able to do; to assisting in giving preassessments, analyzing data, and identifying needs; and teaching small groups using the teacher's lesson plan and recording data to present at student progress meetings to determine student growth.

Contributing to RTI

As discussed in chapter 4 (page 59), RTI is a process that offers every student the additional time and support needed to learn at high levels.

As the first responder to students' needs, educational assistants play a crucial role in giving assessments, analyzing data, and identifying individual students' needs, and—with proper training and understanding of the different tiers of instruction—they can contribute to bridging the gap in student learning. Well-trained educational assistants can give interventions in reading, Leveled Literacy Intervention (https://fountasandpinnell.com/lli), and Bridges Math Intervention (https://math learningcenter.org/curriculum/bridges-intervention). However, including educational assistants requires a thorough training process. At the ICS, the minimum requirement for the position of educational assistant is a bachelor's degree in education. Candidates also take a written exam and experience a thorough interview process. Once they obtain a position, they must take child-protection courses, study the vision and mission of the school, and take continuous professional developments throughout their stay.

Effective RTI implementation requires PLC collaborative teams to implement procedures to do the following.

- Correctly identify students who need intervention.

- Deliver intervention that effectively fills the learning gap for the majority of students exposed to the intervention.

- Monitor the effects of the intervention.

- Make decisions about the type of intervention each student needs.

- Link resulting RTI data to referral for and decisions in special education.

- Link resulting RTI data to system programming change.

There is a direct and irrevocable relationship between how well collaborative teams do these activities and their effects on student learning. To ensure the efficiency of the intervention, schools should include educational assistants in the PLC process. Educational assistants can look at students' postassessment data and see which students need intervention. With the close collaboration of the SST specialist, educational assistants can provide small-group or one-to-one interventions for students. They can also collaboratively look at data from formal and informal assessments to see if the intervention is effective and make decisions to modify the intervention as needed.

When educational assistants are actively involved in PLC conversations, they will be on the same page with teachers regarding student learning, share the responsibility, and take unnecessary pressure off the teacher to ensure every student learns at a high level. The teacher can then focus on transferring student learning, so students make a real-life connection by using their learning to solve real-life problems.

Micro-Teaching

In his book *Visible Learning for Teachers*, Hattie (2012) developed a way of incorporating various influences in different meta-analyses according to their effect size. Hattie (2012) identified factors related to learning outcomes, from positive effects to negative effects. He studied contributing factors such as students, their homes, schools, the curricula, the teacher, and teaching and learning approaches. A review of the evidence finds micro-teaching was the sixth most effective method for improving student outcomes, with a positive effect size of 0.88. *Micro-teaching*, a teacher-training technique for learning teaching skills, employs real teaching situations for developing skills and helps teachers obtain deeper knowledge regarding the art of teaching. This technique involves the steps plan, teach, observe, re-plan, reteach, and re-observe.

During micro-teaching, educational assistants teach a brief lesson to a small group of students. By teaching small, targeted groups, educational assistants bring clarity to complex lessons by limiting and personalizing that whole class–size content and items. They also focus on lessons to develop specific tasks, such as practicing instructional skills. It also allows other educators to reflect and plan improvement.

Guiding Inquiry

The International Baccalaureate Organization (2018) defines the *PYP* as a guided inquiry approach to learning and teaching. Within the PYP, units of inquiry (UI) are the main focus for learning in homeroom classes (classes in which school-specific rather than class-specific activities happen), and teachers integrate UIs into other curriculum areas. Students experience what it looks like to think and act like a writer, reader, historian, scientist, engineer, or mathematician. Within each UI, students and teachers identify what students want to know, their prior knowledge, what they need to know, and how best they might find that out.

In the inquiry-based classroom, there is an emphasis on real-life situations, decision making, problem solving, research, and action. Students are actively exploring, wondering, researching, collecting data, reporting findings, analyzing, and taking action with the guidance of teachers and educational assistants. Figure 6.1 shows the inquiry learning cycle.

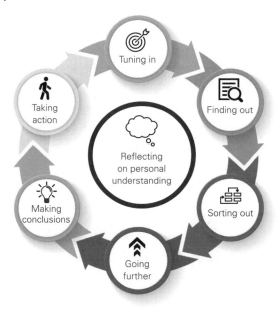

Source: © 2019 by Silicon Valley International School. Adapted with permission.

FIGURE 6.1: The inquiry learning cycle.

Educational assistants can participate in guiding inquiry in each of these elements in the cycle in the following ways.

- **Tuning in:** Educational assistants support students by tuning in to students' thinking and activating their prior knowledge; they design tasks that make students' thinking visible. Educational assistants collect data as students show their prior knowledge through drawings sharing their reflections.

- **Finding out:** Educational assistants think like researchers and gather information from a variety of sources. They challenge students to use research skills to acquire new knowledge. Students use authentic materials to explore concepts through play and experiments.

- **Sorting out:** Students analyze, sort, and categorize information, identifying patterns and making meaning. Educational assistants ask guiding questions and facilitate the small-group conversation as students analyze, sort, and categorize information, identifying patterns and creating meaning. Educational assistants can also provide maps and pictures, books, and other resources that would trigger and foster students' curiosity.

- **Going further:** Educational assistants encourage students to further their inquiry by investigating areas of personal or shared interest. Educational assistants play a significant role in facilitating small groups to work collaboratively to create posters, cards, videos, projects, and so on, expressing their understanding of the unit, taking their learning further, and personalizing how they evidence their learning.

- **Making conclusions:** Educational assistants facilitate student discussions to draw conclusions and make connections between ideas and contexts. After a brief experiment or lesson, educational assistants ask questions and guide students to identify the main findings, note the main limitations relevant to the interpretation of the results, and summarize what the experiment has contributed to the broader understanding of the problem. Educational assistants also record students' findings to identify misconceptions or mastery to inform their teaching.

- **Taking action:** Educational assistants encourage and empower students to apply their learning to new contexts, share with others, and connect with the real world. Educational assistants play a significant role in helping students reflect on their new learning and the implications for personal or shared action. They encourage and empower students to apply their learning to new contexts, share with others, and connect with real-life situations. This might be helping the students identify a real-world problem, reaching out to the community, planning collaboratively to solve this problem, and using students' knowledge to take action.

Leading Literacy

In a balanced literacy framework, students participate in read-alouds, shared reading, guided reading, independent reading, partnerships, and explicit word study instruction using structured word inquiry. In addition, they engage in modeled writing, shared writing, interactive writing, guided writing, and independent writing. The writing process encompasses the writing workshop model. Educational assistants play an important role in conferring and revising the teacher's minilesson, giving interventions and producing documentation to later identify students' needs as a collaborative team, and working in a small group to address individual students' needs with interventions.

Setting Up Classroom Agreements Collaboratively

Every student has the right to learn. Students learn best if their environment has few disturbances. Teachers must provide rules that will ensure learning is positive and each student is treated with respect. Strict adherence to following classroom rules will help ensure students have the best learning environment. Educational assistants can set up classroom agreements in collaboration with the students and the teacher at the beginning of the school year, and then constantly remind students to ensure they live by the agreements. By doing this, educational assistants play a significant role in ensuring safety and student learning at a higher level. As the group of professionals who spend much time with students in the classroom, on the playground, during snacks, and at lunchtime, educational assistants play an important role in keeping students safe, equipping students with conflict-resolution skills, and using positive behavior management strategies.

Creating Smooth Transitions

Educational assistants also play an important role in setting up procedures in the classroom and making sure students follow those procedures at all times. A smooth transition is an extremely important part of classroom management, and educational assistants must be consistent in letting students know all the necessary procedures during class and then follow through. It makes the classroom more organized, therefore the teacher's job becomes easier and less stressful, and it creates a better learning environment for all students. Botched transitions are not only embarrassing but also lose time. If you save fifteen minutes a day through more efficient transitions, it will result in forty-five extra hours of instructional time per year. Therefore, shifting students from one task to the next is worth getting right.

Filling the Gap of Teacher Turnover and Student Transition

Chad Aldeman, policy director with the Edunomics Lab at Georgetown University, conducted a study on teacher turnover in which he says teacher turnover matters, "noting that 'churn [turnover], in general, is a problem, particularly for disadvantaged students'" (as cited in Darling-Hammond, Sutcher, & Carver-Thomas, 2017). IGI Global (n.d.) defines *teacher turnover* as the rate at which teachers exit schools. It consists of both teacher migration (*movers*, those who transfer or migrate to teaching positions in other schools) and teacher attrition (*leavers*, who leave teaching altogether). These rates of turnover are highest in faculties serving low-income students and students of color. Constant churn exacerbates staffing difficulties that result in shortages. Thus, students in these hard-to-staff faculties disproportionately suffer the implications of each turnover and shortage (IGI Global, n.d.; Learning Policy Institute, n.d.).

Aldeman acknowledges, as do I, that the foremost impact of teacher turnover is on students (as cited in Darling-Hammond et al., 2017). Analysis shows that teacher turnover rates negatively impact student accomplishment for all the scholars in every classroom, not simply those in every new teacher's classroom. *Student transition—* students moving from one school to another—also impacts students' learning outcomes negatively (Hattie, 2012).

Educational assistants play a significant role in bridging the gap for new teachers by giving the local context and welcoming to and familiarizing them with the new school, as well as supporting student learning needs resulting from student transition. Educational assistants are helpful to students when there is teacher turnover by giving the consistency of positive teacher-student relationships and trust, setting up the classroom agreement, introducing the school culture, and creating a safe environment.

Conclusion

The conventional education system that prevailed in the manufacturing era is no longer the best learning experience to ensure every student learns at the highest level. The shift from the conventional way of teaching to student-centered learning has made collaboration and personalized learning the new way of doing business in schools. As a result, educational assistants are now actively participating in the classroom and collaborating with other staff in ways that directly and constructively impact student learning.

When it comes to implementation, including educational assistants more deeply in the PLC process in the PYP requires deep conversations among leadership team members to reflect on and change the policies of schools, allocating time for educational assistants to collaborate with the team, and providing professional development for active participation.

Next Steps

Consider the following suggested actions for getting started on becoming highly effective and then moving to the next level by becoming learning progressive.

Getting Started on Being Highly Effective

- Commit to including educational assistants in the PLC process and share the school's mission and vision.

- Provide continuous professional development for educational assistants on the PLC process.

- Have clear guidelines and expectations on the involvement and expectations of educational assistants in the PLC process.

- Create a schedule that authorizes educational assistants to collaborate with teachers and have learning-focused conversations that focus on the four critical questions.

Next Level— Becoming Learning Progressive

- Continue to include educational assistants in the PLC process.

- Provide professional development that equips educational assistants to fully implement the PLC process and ensure students learn at a high level.

> ■ Shift away from a teacher-centered classroom to a more collaborative approach that will allow educational assistants to give students agency.

 # References and Resources

Allen, D. W., & Wang, W. (1996). *Microteaching.* Beijing, China: Xinhua Press.

Blatchford, P., Russell, A., & Webster, R. (2012). *Reassessing the impact of teaching assistants: How research challenges practice and policy.* London: Routledge.

Bronfenbrenner, U. (1979). *The ecology of human development: Experiments by nature and design.* Cambridge, MA: Harvard University Press.

Buffum, A., Mattos, M., & Weber, C. (2012). *Simplifying response to intervention: Four essential guiding principles.* Bloomington, IN: Solution Tree Press.

Darling-Hammond, L., Sutcher, L., & Carver-Thomas, D. (2017, November 8). *Why addressing teacher turnover matters* [Blog post]. Accessed at https://learningpolicyinstitute.org/blog/why-addressing-teacher-turnover-matters on February 28, 2022.

Dillow, C. (2010). *Supporting stories: Being a teaching assistant.* Stoke-on-Trent, England: Trentham Books.

DuFour, R., DuFour, R., Eaker, R., Mattos, M., & Muhammad, A. (2021). *Revisiting Professional Learning Communities at Work: Proven insights for sustained, substantive school improvement* (2nd ed.). Bloomington, IN: Solution Tree Press.

DuFour, R., DuFour, R., Eaker, R., & Many, T. (2010). *Learning by doing: A handbook for Professional Learning Communities at Work* (2nd ed.). Bloomington, IN: Solution Tree Press.

DuFour, R., DuFour, R., Eaker, R., Many, T. W., & Mattos, M. (2016). *Learning by doing: A handbook for Professional Learning Communities at Work* (3rd ed.). Bloomington, IN: Solution Tree Press.

Eaker, R., & Marzano, R. J. (Eds.). (2020). *Professional Learning Communities at Work and High Reliability Schools: Cultures of continuous learning.* Bloomington, IN: Solution Tree Press.

Edwards, C., Gandini, L., & Forman, G. (Eds.). (1998). *The hundred languages of children: The Reggio Emilia Approach—advanced reflections* (2nd ed.). Greenwich, CT: Ablex.

Hattie, J. (2009). *Visible learning: A synthesis of over 800 meta-analyses relating to achievement.* New York: Routledge.

Hattie, J. (2012). *Visible learning for teachers: Maximizing impact on learning.* New York: Routledge.

Hattie, J., & Yates, G. (2014). *Visible learning and the science of how we learn.* London: Routledge, Taylor & Francis.

Herman, K. C., Hickmon-Rosa, J., & Reinke, W. M. (2018). *Empirically derived profiles of teacher stress, burnout, self-efficacy, and coping and associated student outcomes.* Accessed at https://files.eric.ed.gov/fulltext/EJ1173521.pdf on May 21, 2022.

Huitt, W., & Hummel, J. (2003). *Piaget's theory of cognitive development.* Accessed at www.edpsycinteractive.org/topics/cognition/piaget.html on July 14, 2022.

IGI Global. (n.d.). *What is teacher turnover?* Accessed at www.igi-global.com /dictionary/beyond-the-classroom/97405 on May 22, 2022.

International Baccalaureate Organization. (2018). *Learning and teaching in the enhanced PYP.* Accessed at https://blogs.ibo.org/sharingpyp/files/2018/02/2018 -January-Learning-teaching-part-1-ENG.pdf on April 15, 2022.

Jarvis, J. (2019). *Using formative assessment practices to lift student achievement.* Accessed at https://cpl.asn.au/journal/semester-1-2015/using-formative-a ssessment-practices-to-lift-student-achievement on May 21, 2022.

Jaques, D. (1992). *Small group teaching.* Accessed at https://shop.brookes .ac.uk/product-catalogue/oxford-centre-for-staff-learning-development /books-publications/ebooks/small-group-teaching-by-david-jaques-ebook on September 7, 2022.

Jaques, D. (2007). *Learning in groups: A handbook for face-to-face and online environments* (4th ed.). New York: Routledge.

Learning Policy Institute. (n.d.). *Why addressing teacher turnover matters.* Accessed at https://learningpolicyinstitute.org/blog/why-addressing-teacher -turnover-matters on May 22, 2022.

The Open University. (n.d.). *Teaching assistants: Support in action.* Accessed at www .open.edu/openlearn/education-development/education/teaching -assistants-support-action/content-section-4 on May 13, 2022.

Shmis, T., Ambasz, D., & Ustinova, M. (2019, June 26). *Learning environment as third teacher? Evidence on the impact of school infrastructure* [Blog post]. Accessed at https://blogs.worldbank.org/education/learning-environment -third-teacher-evidence-impact-school-infrastructure on May 13, 2022.

Silicon Valley International School. (2019, January 22). *The inquiry learning cycle* [Blog post]. Accessed at https://blog.siliconvalleyinternational.org/the -inquiry-learning-cycle on July 8, 2022.

Staker, H., & Horn, M. B. (2012, May). *Classifying K–12 blended learning.* Accessed at https://files.eric.ed.gov/fulltext/ED535180.pdf on May 22, 2022.

Stuart, T. S. (Ed.). (2016). *Global perspectives: Professional Learning Communities at Work in international schools.* Bloomington, IN: Solution Tree Press.

Stuart, T. S., Heckmann, S., Mattos, M., & Buffum, A. (2018). *Personalized learning in a PLC at Work: Student agency through the four critical questions.* Bloomington, IN: Solution Tree Press.

TeachThought Staff. (n.d.). *28 student-centered instructional strategies.* Accessed at www.teachthought.com/pedagogy/28-student-centered-instructional -strategies on February 28, 2022.

Calley Connelly is elementary school principal at the International Community School (ICS) of Addis Ababa in Ethiopia. She was a mathematics coach and International Baccalaureate (IB) mathematics teacher at the American International School Chennai, where she led the National East South Asia Council Math Collaborative in designing professional learning experiences for mathematics teachers in the near-east region. Calley has been an international school educator since 2002, when she joined the Peace Corps and served as an agroforestry volunteer in the Far North Region of Cameroon and took her first unofficial job as a mathematics teacher. Her educational experiences range from leading a department of one in the American International School of Bamako in Mali, to leading schoolwide mathematics professional learning as a K–12 mathematics coach. Calley's interests as an emerging school leader include diversity, equity, and inclusion in international schools; nurturing trust, well-being, and leadership capacity in PLC team members; and developing a replicable hub model for personalized learning.

Calley is a graduate of Montana Tech of the University of Montana, where she was awarded the Goldwater Scholarship. She earned a master's degree in mathematics and mathematics education from Montana State of the University of Montana. She is pursuing a doctorate in instructional leadership at Wilkes University in Pennsylvania.

To book Calley Connelly for professional development, contact pd@Solution Tree.com.

CHAPTER 7

Leading Change in the PYP Through PLCs

Calley Connelly

If the key tenets of a professional learning community (PLC) are *all students can learn at high levels* and *it's the collective responsibility of all teachers to ensure all students learn at high levels* (DuFour, DuFour, Eaker, Many, & Mattos, 2016), then the key tenets of leadership in a PLC are *all educators can learn at high levels* and *it's the collective responsibility of all leaders to ensure all educators learn at high levels*. If a key aim for International Baccalaureate Primary Years Programme (IB PYP) educators is to help learners develop the attributes in the International Baccalaureate Organization (IBO; 2018c) learner profile, then the key focus for PYP leaders is—you guessed it—to help adult learners develop the attributes in the IB learner profile. As the PYP describes, "When students have agency, the relationship between the teacher and students becomes a partnership. Students with a strong sense of self-efficacy bring a stronger sense of agency to the learning community" (IBO, 2018c). Why make artificial distinctions between the need for agency in younger learners and adult learners? The elementary leadership team members at the International Community School (ICS) of Addis Ababa in Ethiopia work from the premise that when educators have agency, the relationship between educators and leaders becomes a partnership. The team works hard to develop a sense of self-efficacy in adult learners, and to give them a stronger sense of agency in designing their learning community.

This chapter expands on how the four critical questions of a PLC and the IB learner profile inform the practices as an elementary school leadership team. What kind of leadership is needed to effect change and growth using the PLC process in a PYP learning environment? How do leaders in this context see themselves and their teams through the sea change of becoming collaborative and concept focused, and leaning into personalization and agency as teams of educators? I will examine ICS's leadership practices and scenarios through a theory of professional and personal adult development, and share some strategies when incorporating these approaches for leaders. Finally, I will consider the next steps and pervasive challenges in ICS's leadership journey.

The Leadership Team as a Collaborative Team

An elementary school leadership team is most focused, most effective, and most learner centered when members work together as a collaborative team. Ideally, in a PLC, leaders would establish a fractal collaborative team model in which every team—from the leadership team to the early years 2 team—is asking and answering the four critical questions, tailored to their "class of educators" (Timperley, 2011). Leaders must be conscientious and ensure they are not too narrowly focused on the development of individual principals, teachers, or educational assistants that they forget to attend to the professional learning needs of the community of adult learners as a whole. The ICS elementary school leadership team asked University of Auckland professor emerita Helen Timperley's (2011) fantastic question, "Who is my class?" Team members identified two core "classes," for whose learning and growth they are directly responsible (not indirectly, as for student learning and growth): the early years and elementary school educators and the team leaders. Thus, our leadership team's modified four critical questions (DuFour et al., 2016) are as follows.

1. What do we want all educators (or team leaders) to understand, know, and be able to do?

2. How will we know if they have learned it?

3. How will we respond when some educators (or team leaders) do not learn?

4. How will we extend the learning for educators (or team leaders) who are already proficient?

The four PLC critical questions guided the team through the more straightforward curricula of new-hire orientation, all-faculty in-service training, and strategic planning with the office of learning for the early years and elementary school educators. Less obviously, considering the team leaders' professional growth, the four questions helped ICS implement a strategic approach to team leader meeting time that addresses the capacity-building needs of team leaders and honors their growth as true leaders, not just managers.

Our elementary school leadership team worked hard to plan a strategic team leader curriculum. To develop this curriculum, members first answered critical question one by examining the team leader's job description and operationalizing it into indicators for team leader success (see figure 7.1).

Job Description Highlights	Actions	Indicators for Survey
To be a mid-level leader in the elementary school by actively supporting all leadership decisions within the team To hold the team accountable to all leadership decisions	To support the principals' and leadership team decisions To represent the PLC views, interests, and needs to the principals	I represent the needs of my team openly to the leadership team. I actively support decisions from the leadership team in team meetings. I hold my team accountable for all leadership team decisions and action items.
To lead the team in supporting the ICS collaborative commitments To lead collaboration among team members	To model and promote collaborative teaching practices To follow the seven norms of collaboration in meetings and address any team concerns To ask the four PLC questions to guide discussions To promote teamwork and to motivate staff to ensure effective working relations	I lead my team's collaboration using our norms and the PLC process guidelines. I promote teamwork and motivate my colleagues to ensure effective working relations.
To be a positive and motivating influence on the collaborative team To be accountable for curriculum and assessment development within the grade level or specialty	To work with all coaches in the ICS office of learning To work with the elementary school principals to identify staff development needs To produce and save all meeting agendas and notes—or assign a team member to this task To ensure the team's PYP documentation is complete To report grade-level and specialist progress toward all elementary schoolwide goals	I am a positive and motivating influence on the team. I model openness in coaching and collaboration with my learning coach, PYP coordinator, and supervisor. I hold my team accountable to make sure our PYP documentation is complete. I develop and facilitate agendas that support team collaboration.

Source: © 2021 by the International Community School of Addis Ababa. Adapted with permission.

FIGURE 7.1: Team leader job description operationalized into self-assessment indicators.

continued ➔

Job Description Highlights	Actions	Indicators for Survey
To actively support the development of the IB PYP To ensure the provision of an appropriately broad, balanced, relevant, and differentiated curriculum for students in the grade level or special education in accordance with the mission and strategic plan of the school, as well as the requirements of the PYP	To schedule and assign meeting time with specialists, student support team, English as an additional language team, counselors, and others as needed To develop learning activities, assessment practices, and teaching and learning strategies that support personalized learning (student agency) in the grade level or specialist area To coordinate orders for resources and prepare all grade-level purchase orders	I actively lead the development of learning activities, assessments, and strategies that support personalized learning. I effectively coordinate orders for resources.

Team leaders then self-assessed using a Likert scale against the indicators and added comments to support their ratings and other support needs. Principals cross-checked some of these self-assessments through hub observations and participation in collaborative team meeting time. The leadership team prioritized the needs for team leader learning and identified outliers who needed individualized support. Finally, the team moved away from a weekly team leader managerial meet-up to a rotating schedule that alternates between operational topics and explicit professional learning.

Next, the team addressed the second critical question, How will we know if the team leaders have learned these new strategies, and are applying them in a leadership capacity on their collaborative teams? Members knew that traditional teacher observations wouldn't cut it. "Supervising individual teachers into better performance is impossible if you have a staff of, say, more than 20 teachers," suggests Michael Fullan (2014), global leadership director of New Pedagogies for Deep Learning, in *The Principal* (p. 40). With a staff of 115 educators in the early years and elementary section of the school, team members knew they would have to apply creative strategies to their assessment approach.

In this case, the team's focus was about measuring the success of the team leader both as an individual and how well the leader transfers learning to the entire team. For individual team leaders, the leadership team established a one-to-one weekly check-in with the supervising principal to open a dialogue about successes and challenges. This dialogue, especially in its consistency and nonjudgmental coaching nature, allows team leaders to be vulnerable and express challenges and successes openly. For establishing the transfer of skills and understandings to the teams, members modified some of the strategies from *Trust-Based Observations* (Randall, 2020) to develop a collective hub observation approach that honors the interdependence of the team members while providing clear expectations and direct feedback to each individual (see figure 7.2). Richard DuFour and Robert Marzano (2009) note that time devoted to building the capacity of teachers to work in teams is far better spent than the time devoted to observing individual teachers. The nonprescriptive nature of the observation (that is, focusing on observable strengths of each team member) honors each individual's agency while provoking meaningful conversations among the whole hub group. The observation also allows the principal to assess up to eight educators working with up to eight flexible groups of students (see an example in figure 7.2). This is a time-efficient method for the principals to give whole-group feedback; the data are a valuable third point for team reflection. As DuFour and Marzano (2009) suggest, this is time more effectively spent in developing the group capacity rather than developing the capacity of individual teachers.

Elementary School Hub Bubble Observation
Date _____ **Time** _____ **Subject** _____
Grade-Level Goals [Link] *Add grade-level goals from preceding link.* • What were your question one goals for students or groups? • With these question one data, how did your team decide on these learning opportunities for students? • How did your team decide on roles and responsibilities for these engagements? • If you had it all to do over again, how might you change your strategies to personalize for student learning?
Educator Names and Roles: Note which educators are present and the roles of each (for example: small-group leader, large-group leader, lesson support, co-teaching, individual attention, circulating, data gathering, planning, unclear, other)
Teacher and Student Rapport and Relationship: Note evidence of positive teacher-student rapport (for example: one-to-ones; tone; humor; respect; teacher sharing of themselves; student sharing of themselves; teacher sharing mistakes; empathy; knowledge of individual student; body language; accountability; high expectations; feedback to students; active listening; use of encouragement versus praise; evidence of student agency; teacher-to-teacher rapport)

Source: © 2021 by the International Community School of Addis Ababa. Adapted with permission.

FIGURE 7.2: Hub observation form.

continued →

Classroom Culture for Learning: Note positive evidence of classroom culture (for example: accountable voice; cold-calling; choices; strong class beginnings; short lessons and teacher talk; proximity; strong transitions; responsive teaching; cooperative learning; interventions, extensions, clear expectations, and directions; students displaying understanding of routines; consequences)

Formative Assessment and Knowing What Each Student Learned to Guide Next Steps: Note each adult who enacted which strategies for assessment (for example: interviews; conferring; pair and share; graphic organizers; exit slips; exemplars: demonstration station; examples and non-examples; mini-whiteboards; three things; analogy; draw it; Venn diagram; non-graded quizzes; self- and peer assessment)

Spaces: Note the strategic use of space (for example: mountain top, cave, watering hole, campfire, hands-on, movement, student community work, anchor charts, flexible groupings, organized mess, aesthetically inviting, purposeful use of spaces, spaces for individual or group use)

Questioning: Note educators' use of questioning strategies (for example stems such as *might, could, possibly, wonder, teacher question, student question, questions posted, questions* or *resources referred to, questions explored, open questions, closed questions*).

Suggestions, Questions, Other Data:

Visit go.SolutionTree.com/PLCbooks for a free reproducible version of this figure.

With regard to question three, How will we respond if some educators (or team leaders) do not learn?, it is important to note that this form (figure 7.2, page 143) does not address significant deviations from expectations. Rather, the team's aim is to personalize its feedback and interventions for adult learners in need of support, just as team members expect the adult learners to do for individual students. The team offers principals or curriculum and coaching support with PYP coordinators to teachers and educational assistants in need of support mentorship. In the case of deep concerns, the team attends to educators' professional growth needs through a structured professional improvement plan that aligns with schoolwide collaborative commitments.

How do we support our exceptionally skilled team leaders and educators? As team members ask question four, How will we extend the learning for educators (team leaders) who are already proficient?, they start by establishing some opportunities for networking with the early years and elementary school team members. Once team members identify a team leader or collaborative team member successfully implementing one of the team's key strategies, members look for opportunities to send colleagues to visit his or her classroom. This can look very informal, such as a collegial walkthrough, or it could be as formal as a learning walk in collaboration with a PYP coordinator or principal. The leadership team members also believe in the power of teacher-led professional learning; and while this is not an established practice in the elementary school, strategy-sharing in the team leader meetings or among the online leaders has made an impact on teams that had felt stuck and isolated due to COVID protocols. Finally, the team offers proficient team leaders and other educators opportunities to share their learning more widely; some of the most skilled colleagues are leading PYP and concept-based curriculum and instruction workshops around the world, as well as presenting with the International Schools Association. The elementary school leadership team is proud of its teachers' success and encourages them to share widely by offering travel funding for presenting, as well as professional leave.

The Adult Learner Profile

In the previous section, I attended to *how* members work as a leadership team to develop adult learners. In this section, I focus on *what* leadership teams develop and *why* it is so deeply important to the professional learning and growth for all stakeholders. I make connections to the IB learner profile and illustrate how the choices of a leadership team intend to support the development of educators using the adult learner profile.

The IB learner profile "represents a broad range of human capacities and responsibilities that encompass intellectual, personal, emotional and social growth" (IBO, 2018c). The ten attributes that leaders aim to embody, and to develop in young and adult learners, are "Inquirers, Knowledgeable, Thinkers, Communicators, Principled, Open-minded, Caring, Risk-takers, Balanced, and Reflective" (IBO, 2018c). The IBO (2018c) goes further to explain that "students with a strong sense of self-efficacy bring a stronger sense of agency to the learning community." While the IBO's (2018b) research and philosophy focus on student learning, other research corroborates the ways in which self-efficacy is a means and an end to personal development. Coauthors William Powell and Ochan Kusuma-Powell (2015) establish that successful development as a collaborative team member involves developing self-directedness, cooperativeness, and self-transcendence, character traits that affect the member's identities as an educator and human being. Powell and Kusuma-Powell (2015) further describe the bidirectional effect of character on experience, stating, "character influences our perception of life experiences and those experiences in turn influence the development of character . . . none of these are fixed" (p. 39). At ICS, the elementary leadership members' belief as learning-focused school leaders is that the opportunity to participate in a well-functioning collaborative team can be instrumental to the self-actualization of individual educators. The responsibility of leaders is to set the conditions for this growth and development for collaborative team members, just as it is the collaborative team members' responsibility to set the conditions for students. What follows are some real examples of leadership scenarios and beliefs that align with each of the learner profile attributes.

Caring: Develop a Culture of Equity and Inclusion

ISC's journey to become a PLC required the elementary leadership team members to examine how they engage with their collaborating adult learners. Members realized they were not honoring the voices of all of the educators in the room with an educational assistant model (see chapter 6, page 121, for a discussion of this model). Local hires in the educational assistant role contribute a crucial element of institutional memory and local context; had the team sidelined these colleagues as just helpers, members would miss out on their perspective. Team members made moves to more intentionally acknowledge, value, and professionally grow these colleagues.

These changes started with surface-level impacts; for example, changing the job title from *teacher's assistant* to *educational assistant* and improving compensation. The team also shifted to a daily planning approach that allows educational assistants to participate as full members of the collaborative team, asking and answering the four critical questions of a PLC with their teacher colleagues. Some of the deeper changes have been more transformational; for example, including educational assistants in formal PYP training and balancing teacher and educational assistant duties (such as playground time) more equitably. Going forward, the team members are identifying pathways to international certification and equitable hiring practices that would allow more representation of local colleagues in a lead teaching role.

Knowledgeable: Build Leadership Team Capacity, Deep and Wide

Many PYP schools with a traditional structure include a single PYP coordinator, responsible for the units of inquiry for early years through grade 5. With ICS's personalized learning PLC context, the elementary leadership team members knew it was possible to develop more subject- and grade-level-specific understanding with better facilitation of collaborative teams. Thus, members decided on a model that includes two PYP coordinators, each with a full range of curricular responsibilities and deep knowledge of all subject areas for their grade levels. Team members also restructured their *coaches cadre* to be fully integrated. With two PYP coordinators, one for lower elementary and one for upper elementary, along with a dedicated early years coordinator, it is reasonable to ask these individuals to take on mathematics and literacy alignment and lead the collaborative teams' conversations once weekly for units of inquiry and once weekly for mathematics or literacy. The team reduced the early years' workload of the lower elementary coordinator and identified clear responsibilities for each coordinator regarding specialists. In the short term, this work improved collaborative team accountability and the quality of curriculum alignment and documentation; in the long term, team members anticipate seeing improvement in the integration of mathematics and literacy into units of inquiry.

Communicator: Attend to Team Development Early and Often

As the ICS elementary leadership team members moved toward hub learning, one thing became immediately clear: the explicit development of teams is crucial to success. Each team has eight to twelve adults, with at least three members in roles of teacher, student support teacher, and educational assistant. These members provide eight to twelve different points of view, worldviews, backgrounds, and at least two sets of cultural communication norms (American and Ethiopian). While ICS communities encompass many third-culture adults, two of Dutch social psychologist Geert Hofstede's (2011) cultural dimensions are markedly distinct for the two dominant cultures of American and host-country educators. First, *individualism*, the degree of interdependence a society maintains among its members, is rated 91 for the United States and 20 for the ICS host country (Ethiopia). Second, *power distance*, the extent to which the less-powerful members of institutions and organizations in a country expect and accept that power is distributed unequally, is rated 40 for the United States and 70 for Ethiopia. Combined, these two imbalances allow the team to generalize (not specify, since each individual's traits vary markedly within any culture) that the members' American colleagues are likely to engage openly without regard for hierarchy and want input on all decisions, while the local Ethiopian colleagues seek role clarity and defer to perceived hierarchy. To combat these differences and level the collaborative playing field, the team needed explicit norms and structures in place to ensure full participation (Garmston, 2002).

Furthermore, cultural differences are only one layer of challenges. Personality-based challenges also emerge. The team identified the following strategies to help team leaders explicitly develop the other teams, leaving very little to chance. At the beginning of the year, team members ask all new faculty to take a brief strengths assessment; all returning faculty participated the prior year. Members then used the High5Test (2021) strengths results as a leadership exercise with team leaders. Elementary leadership team members facilitated a session called *What's Right With You?* in which members modeled unpacking team strengths, using a behavior-profiling tool (Lencioni, 2012). The team leaders took the resources and facilitated the same session with their collaborative teams. The follow-up was a deep dive into norms of collaboration, and then a conversation about reminders and conflicting styles, asking collaborative team members, "How do you like to be reminded?" Team leaders and individual team members reflected with the leadership team so these strategies positively impact team development schoolwide.

Inquirer and Thinker: Ask, Then Listen for Patterns

As principal of a PYP and PLC school, it's been crucial for me to take the time to meet one-to-one with each of the educators. These meetings should be short and inquiry based, with just enough guidance to encourage educators each to open up about their background, professional growth with the school, and their successes, challenges, and suggestions. I've asked each person, "What is something special about our school that we should never change?" and followed up with, "And what is something that we *must* change?"

The benefits of these one-to-one meetings have been immeasurable. First, I underestimated the opportunity for authentic connection with each of the adult learners. It's been truly heartwarming to find out more about my colleagues: more about their families, their journeys, how an inquiry-based approach to teaching and learning influences their philosophies about parents. It's also been heart-wrenching to hear them speak about the challenges that affect their well-being and effectiveness in the classroom. While each individual interview has been an opportunity for connection and learning, overall, the notes from my comprehensive one-to-one meetings form a body of data that will impact the leadership team's decisions going forward. As a caring inquirer, I empathize with each individual's situation and concerns. As a thinking principal, I know I must move beyond the specifics and look for patterns to determine how our school can improve in the ways that meet educators' needs and impact student learning.

Balanced and Reflective: Create a Culture of Reasonable Expectations and Reflective Practice

Change toward personalization has not been easy, but ICS leaders use a mantra of "Don't let perfect get in the way of progress." Instead of using a supervision or expectations rubric on which teams and individuals would want to be meeting or exceeding, the ICS leaders developed a learning and teaching continuum (see figure 7.3, page 150) for growing as personalized learning practitioners. Members had to acknowledge significant challenges to implementation. For example, the team's purpose-built hub building had to be divided into two classrooms to meet COVID-19 safety precautions, and many ICS teachers experienced mental and physical health challenges. Leaders asked teams to self-assess openly on the continuum without judging their current status. Leaders also reiterated with teams, "The goal is not to reach the far end of the continuum this year—in our current context it is not even possible! But rather, the goal is to identify areas in which each team can improve and move forward on the continuum."

ICS Elementary School Learning and Teaching Continuum, 2020–2021				
Criteria	**Traditional**	**Emerging**	**Invested**	**Innovative Full-Hub Model**
Goal One: Health and Well-Being				
Implement COVID guidelines.	Enforce playbook rules (link to playbook).	Model and develop student understanding of playbook.	Encourage and assist with developing student leadership of health and safety.	Engage students in designing health innovations.
Support student well-being.	Refer struggling students to counselor.	Develop a welcoming community of learners. Recognize that student well-being takes priority over academic needs in times of crisis.	Proactively address and support social-emotional needs of the school community. Establish consistent approaches to creating conditions that empower students' self-esteem and self-image.	Personalize and deliver collaborative learning experiences to foster social-emotional literacy. Create consistent and respectful understanding of differences and setting of limits. Provide structures for students to self-advocate and take ownership over their well-being and the well-being of others.
Support colleague well-being.	Be professional and kind. Have personal awareness that we are all different as international teachers, and there will be challenges to overcome.	Be a supportive member of my team. In what ways can I be a supportive team member?	Be an encouraging and supportive member of school teams and the broader ICS community. Recognize when I need to be empathetic and reflect on practices.	Proactively identify and support well-being needs of colleagues and the community. Recognize when others need support and offer it.

Goal Two: Building Relationships			
Use a collaborative team approach.	Teachers work independently.	Teachers collaborate with like-minded colleagues on basic planning tasks, avoiding team conflict. Understand others may not be like-minded.	Teachers and educational assistants collaborate on learning targets and assessments, working through team conflict, with support if necessary.	Teachers and educational assistants collaborate and release responsibilities across the community to plan, evaluate student data, and reflect; the team embraces cognitive conflict to find best solutions.
Build relationships with students.	Teachers develop and maintain respectful relationships with students. Acknowledge that students, teachers, and families will have different beliefs about learning.	Teachers learn more about their students (for example, family, friends, interests, strengths, challenges) and begin to develop respectful and positive relationships irrespective of differences.	Teachers and students know one another well and begin to form partnerships. When facing challenges, teachers can use effective strategies to support students. Teachers develop relationships with families and students, acknowledging differences in family dynamics by learning to be flexible and tolerant.	Teacher and student mutual understanding and trust lead to effective, open communication and student-led learning. Teachers collaborate with families to build common understandings and work collaboratively to support individual student learning opportunities.

Source: © 2021 by the International Community School of Addis Ababa. Adapted with permission.

FIGURE 7.3: Example of learning and teaching continuum.

The teams each self-assessed collaboratively, highlighting their current and desired status. Teams identify a few key goals for improvement, and principals provide direct coaching on these goals. At the end of the semester and year, teams individually reflect on their group and individual progress toward these goals. Teams even reflect on the process, and these meta-reflections have helped the ICS elementary leadership team identify that the continuum and the trust-based self-assessment and coaching have made improvement more accessible and measurable for all educators.

Principled: Take a Stand About What's Tight and What's Loose

A personalized learning leadership team is asking for a great deal of flexibility and resilience from teachers. Members need teachers to anticipate student misunderstandings, plan to meet a wide range of needs, and respond to students in the moment with instructional agility. One of the ICS elementary leadership team beliefs is that teams are most successful when external expectations are clear (Catalyft Success System, 2016). Educator agency is then economized for high-impact decisions such as instructional strategies and responding to assessment data. As a leadership team, members take on the responsibility and challenge to define and communicate expectations. The leadership challenge in this context has been developing models from teachers' on-the-ground learning that are transferable to other hubs. One big takeaway from year one in personalized learning hubs has been the importance of models, and this remains an area for growth since ICS is developing its own models, not following any scripts.

Risk-Taker: Try Something New When Something New Is Needed

In the movie *Back to the Future* (Zemeckis, 2009), Dr. Emmett Brown says, "Where we are going, we won't need roads," as he and Marty McFly head into the future in Brown's car-based time machine (which, in the movie, was 2015). Jumping into that flying car must've been a little bit scary! As a leadership team, members must get ready for what's next and model risk taking to other teams. However, this requires innovative authentic provocations, not just change for change's sake.

One challenge most PYP schools experience is the meaningful integration of specialists into units of inquiry. This is especially vital for PLC schools in which collaborative team time is so crucial for developing conceptual understandings of the units. Whenever students were in specials, their homeroom teachers were planning.

It proved challenging for four specialists to collaborate effectively with three teams to integrate. The leadership team felt stymied until members decided to think outside the box, shrink expectations in one dimension, and grow them in another, and then try something completely new. Voilà, Global Wednesdays!

The key features of Global Wednesdays are single specialist integration, increased language and host-country learning, and a team-teaching model for specialists and homeroom teachers. On Wednesdays, each specialist joins only one team for the whole school day. Instead of pull-out specialist learning on that day, the specialists each integrate their subject-area–related concepts into the whole day. Leaders encourage teams to invite the specialist as a *whole person*, meaning that specialists each bring their whole self to the team, not just their specialist skills. French teachers still teach French, which gives students French class three times weekly; the desired outcome here is improved language acquisition by adding an extra class every two weeks. Finally, the team reintroduced Amharic language and Ethiopian studies as the second specialist class on Global Wednesdays to bolster students' international mindedness and to offer educational assistants a leadership opportunity.

This year during ICS's accreditation visit from IB and the Council of International School's (CIS), leaders received repeated commendations about Global Wednesday. Parents in the ICS community chat room were raving about the changes. How did the leadership team pull off such a big sweeping change, and so successfully? First, members took something off the plate: they eliminated all morning duty for specialists and added support for specialists' lunch duty on Wednesdays. Second, the team built in an on-ramp: the first three Wednesdays of the school year were regular Wednesdays but after that, the time was professional planning time for specialists to plan with their new teams. Third, the team intentionally scaffolded team members to get to know the tools mentioned previously. The team still needs to refine this model, to decide when to mix up collaborations and how to support each team to be successful, but members can see this risk has paid dividends.

Open-Minded: All Hands on Deck

During the first weeks of the new normal of COVID-19 restrictions, my collaborating principal and I joked that "no one is working at their paygrade." As a principal, I was taping *X*s to cafeteria tables for social distancing, the head of school was helping move furniture around hubs, and teachers were taking temperatures at the gate. Although these particular circumstances were without precedent, the need for all stakeholders to adapt quickly to unforeseen events is not exceptional. If you want a PYP and PLC with personalized learning to succeed, it's going to take a lot of collaboration to make it happen. Principals can lead subject reviews, and curriculum coordinators can coach too, plus counselors can integrate into the grade-level teams. Staff all cover for and learn from one another. Leaders' presence in the classroom or during new initiatives elevates the dynamic and maintains progress.

 Conclusion

Leading a PYP and PLC school is an inquiry unto itself. Navigating the challenges of a learning-progressive personalized learning context with a hub model, while keeping the focus on highly effective learning, means juggling many complexities. Humble leadership must be your default in this novel and ever-changing context. ICS leadership team members identify first as *learners*—as the lead learners in a community focused on learning. Educators believe all students can learn, and leaders believe all educators can learn and grow. Leaders nurture the talents and intellect of each adult learner as these educators move forward to impact students in their classrooms.

 Next Steps

Consider the following suggested actions for getting started on becoming highly effective and then moving to the next level by becoming learning progressive.

Getting Started on Being Highly Effective

- Audit your decision-making processes. Where can you create more opportunities for teacher agency, not only in classroom decisions but also in sectional (departmental) decisions?

- Invest in your team leaders with internal or external leadership professional learning. After all, they are your "class."

- Ask every member of your team, "How have you grown at our school? What makes our school special? What should we stop doing?" Then *listen*.

Moving to the Next Level—Becoming Learning Progressive

- Move from a proficiency-based rubric to a growth continuum for your informal observations. Share positive evidence of growth, as well as next steps, with teachers and teams.

- Find ways to get specialists into your homerooms for real-time co-teaching and collaboration. Think outside the box and commit to an authentic transdisciplinary experience.

- Join each member of your leadership team to self-assess and self-describe according to the IB learner profile. Which descriptions seem forced? Which resonate? Acknowledge the diversity and strengths of each team member and let the learner profile guide your leadership team's next steps.

 # References and Resources

Catalyft Success System. (2016). *Delegation and managing using the tight-loose-tight model.* Accessed at https://irp-cdn.multiscreensite.com/b5849e19 /files/uploaded/Delegation%20and%20Managing%20Using%20the%20 Tight%20-%20Loose%20-%20Tight%20Model.pdf on May 20, 2022.

DuFour, R., DuFour, R., Eaker, R., Many, T. W., & Mattos, M. (2016). *Learning by doing: A handbook for Professional Learning Communities at Work* (3rd ed.). Bloomington, IN: Solution Tree Press.

DuFour, R., & Marzano, R. J. (2009). How teachers learn: High-leverage strategies for principal leadership. *Educational Leadership, 66*(5), 62–68. Accessed at https://ascd.org/el/articles/high-leverage-strategies-for-principal-leadership on July 11, 2022.

Fullan, M. (2014). *The principal: Three keys to maximizing impact.* San Francisco: Jossey-Bass.

Garmston, R. J. (2002). The 5 principles of successful meetings. *The Learning System, 1*(4), 1, 6–8.

High5Test. (2021). *Discover the best part of yourself.* Accessed at https://high5test.com on May 20, 2022.

Hofstede, G. (2011). Dimensionalizing cultures: The Hofstede model in context. *Online Readings in Psychology and Culture, 2*(1). Accessed at https://doi .org/10.9707/2307-0919.1014 on July 26, 2022.

International Baccalaureate Organization. (2018a). *Collaborative planning process for learning and teaching.* Accessed at https://xmltwo.ibo.org/publications /PYP/p_0_pypxx_pip_1810_1/pdf/collaborative-planning-process-en.pdf on July 26, 2022.

International Baccalaureate Organization. (2018b). *Learning and teaching.* Accessed at https://resources.ibo.org/data/learning-and-teaching_899fc563-3f16 -4ad6-89c7-f60983c9d6d3/learning-and-teaching-en_bffd8f20-78b3-4d6e -83dc-7255d1bf1c29.pdf on July 26, 2022.

International Baccalaureate Organization. (2018c). *The learner.* Accessed at https://resources.ibo.org/data/the-learner_fc17a71a-2344-4b26-84cb -caca3a02750d/the-learner-en_d32875a1-8611-4de3-9f7d-14a22127adc2 .pdf on July 26, 2022.

Lencioni, P. (2012). *The advantage: Why organizational health trumps everything else in business.* San Francisco: Jossey-Bass.

Powell, W., & Kusuma-Powell, O. (2015). *Teacher self-supervision: Why teacher evaluation has failed and what we can do about it.* Melton, Woodbridge, England: Catt Educational.

Randall, C. (2020). *Trust-based observations.* New York: Rowman & Littlefield.

Timperley, H. (2011). *Realizing the power of professional learning.* New York: Open University Press.

Zemeckis, R. (Director). (1985). *Back to the future* [Motion picture]. United States: Universal Pictures.

Afterword

Timothy S. Stuart and David (Cal) Callaway

For generations, educators have strived to do their best for each student in their care. Over time, governments, researchers, and a variety of cultural and historical movements have shaped both large-scale shifts in educational approaches and smaller, more local changes in classroom practice. Through all these changes, current thinking has brought educators to some clear and important anchors in how they now support students' learning. Most essentially, educators need an approach to education that is both highly effective *and* learning progressive. Regardless of the specific learning outcomes or curricular framework your school uses, it is important to not only make sure you are highly effective at ensuring students demonstrate mastery of the intended learning outcomes but also learning progressive in your approach, allowing students to take ownership of their own learning, and learning *how to learn* by supporting their agency. Agency and self-efficacy are fundamental to learning in the International Baccalaureate Primary Years Programme (IB PYP). The framework supports learners as agents for their own and others' learning. Learners direct their learning with a strong sense of identity and self-belief, and in conjunction with others, build a sense of community and awareness for the opinions, values, and needs of others (International Baccalaureate Organization, n.d.).

The High Reliability Schools™ model supports schools to become highly effective and learning progressive. We recommend the book *Professional Learning Communities at Work and High Reliability Schools* (Eaker & Marzano, 2020) for schools looking to help students learn at the highest levels. Schools adopting an IB PYP framework together with the professional learning community (PLC) process can support the five levels in the High Reliability Schools model and also support schools in reaching the highest levels of learning and engagement for their students.

Our hope is that this book provides you with a clear and compelling case for how the IB PYP framework and PLC process are not only compatible constructs but also enhance each other in the goal of ensuring high levels of learning and engagement. Each chapter gives detailed examples, structures, and strategies to move your school forward when working to develop both programs in your school context; the next steps at the end of each chapter provide you with provocations for conversations to have as a team within your schools. We hope this book inspires you to provide high levels of learning for all students through agency, inquiry, and collaboration—*a personalized and agentic pedagogy of with.*

 # References

Eaker, R., & Marzano, R. J. (Eds.). (2020). *Professional Learning Communities at Work and High Reliability Schools: Cultures of continuous learning.* Bloomington, IN: Solution Tree Press.

International Baccalaureate Organization. (n.d.). *Primary Years Programme.* Accessed at www.ibo.org/about-the-ib/mission on May 14, 2022.

Index

159

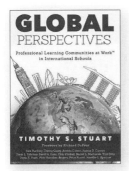

Global Perspectives
Timothy S. Stuart

Tailored specifically to international schools, this resource will guide you through every aspect of PLC implementation. The book's contributors are all international-school educators who have successfully recultured their schools into PLCs. They offer strategies and techniques for taking your school from good to great.
BKF713

Leading PLCs at Work® Districtwide
Robert Eaker, Mike Hagadone, Janel Keating, and Meagan Rhoades

Ensure your district is doing the right work, the right way, for the right reasons. With this resource as your guide, you will learn how to align the work of every PLC team districtwide— from the boardroom to the classroom.
BKF942

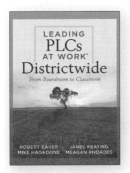

Learning by Doing
Richard DuFour, Rebecca DuFour, Robert Eaker, Thomas W. Many, and Mike Mattos

This book is an action guide for closing the knowing-doing gap and transforming schools into PLCs. It includes seven major additions that equip educators with essential tools for confronting challenges.
BKF416

Taking Action: A Handbook for RTI at Work™
Austin Buffum, Mike Mattos, and Janet Malone

This comprehensive implementation guide covers every element required to build a successful RTI at Work™ program in schools. The authors share step-by-step actions for implementing the essential elements, the tools needed to support implementation, and tips for engaging and supporting educators.
BKF684